1600+
SUPER INTERESTING FUN
FACTS
FOR CURIOUS SMART
MINDS

PAUL DEV

ISBN-13: 9798346941828

Cover design by: Ayyash Publishing Ltd

1600+ SUPER INTERESTING FUN FACTS FOR CURIOUS SMART MINDS

Educational Knowledge Trivia Book of Science, History & Others
for Kid Teen Tween Preteeen Boys Girls Adults

PAUL DEV

CONTENTS

INTRODUCTION

Get ready to dive into an ocean of amazement, where you will find things, you never knew!

Are you ready to tear into the world of interesting facts?

Do you know that *giraffes can swim*? Or, did you know, *you cannot write someone's name with red ink in North Korea*? Have you ever heard that *the original Monopoly board was circular*?

Yes, we are here to unveil such amazing secrets. This book is a fantastic collection of **1600+ facts** for inquisitive adults. At the same time, it is an amazing tool for curious little champs to read, learn, and play. You can share the strange and hidden knowledge of the universe with your fellas, like:

- Hummingbirds' nests are so small that they resemble walnuts in size.

- If you are blindfolded, you will naturally walk in a circular pattern instead of straight.

- Every year, an average of 100 people choke to death while using ballpoint pens.

Facts like these and hundreds of more astonishing trivial information are waiting for you. Open the book and dive into the world of amazing information.

I have gathered top-of-the-line facts to satisfy your innate curiosity. In this book, you will find a wide range of topics covering almost every field of life like animals, building, country, plants, the universe, food, comics, games, science, weather, and so much more. This Educational Trivia & Fun Facts Book brings to you:

- **1600+** accurate, reliable and interesting facts.

- A **wide range of topics and sub-topics** arranged in alphabetical order

- **36 main chapters** are further divided into sub-chapters to keep things organized and findable.

- A **minimum of 20 facts** in each chapter.

- Easy and simple language for **kids**.

Knowledge is power! These facts are not just for fun but a great source to have a better understanding of things around you, your body, different cultures, and technology. The information you will get from this book will also help you in your studies, exams, and presentations. You can support your answers by quoting the facts and impressing your teacher with your out-of-the-course knowledge.

If you are among those intellectuals who get excited about hearing mysterious and exciting things, this is your go-to book. You will be amazed to learn that pearls melt in vinegar, blind people see visuals in dreams, blue in colors, and roses in flowers are the most favorite worldwide.

There are countless ways you can make use of these facts. For instance, with the help of these facts, you can:

- **Arrange a quiz** for your family and friends. Ask them questions and give gifts to the winner – a great round of applause will also do!

- **Win a trivial competition** conducted by your school, an organization, or probably on TV.

- **Start a conversation** with a newcomer in your class, a guest at your home, or a friend in the park.

- **Enjoy your free time** in reading and exploring the hidden truths of the world.

- **Make the most out of your long drives**, enjoy a rainy day, or relax on a beach.

Whether you are a nature lover, an astrophile, a gamer, or curious about the features of the Earth, I have got you covered. You can jump to your favorite topic and read it before other chapters. Amazingly, reading facts can help you in several ways. For example:

- Trivia helps to **improve memory**, as it is a workout for your brain.

- It **improves your learning** and boosts knowledge.

- It makes you **feel happier** and positively affects your mood.

- It provides you with a chance to spend time with your friends and family, which ultimately **improves your mental health**.

- You get a **better idea about the origins** and histories and link the previous information to fill the gaps in between.

- Trivia keeps the mind busy in a **healthy activity**.

So, what are you waiting for? It is time to sit back and delve into an exciting journey. Explore the universe fact by fact. From history to geography, games to vocabulary, and military to religion, you will enjoy every color and every taste of this book. Let's get started!

ANIMAL

- [ ] Certain animals have the innate ability to regenerate missing body parts, including tails and limbs.

- [ ] The hydra is renowned for its capacity to regenerate tissues and cells, due to this, it seems to be immune to death.

- [ ] Although some 230,000 marine species have been recognized, it's thought that up to two million more are yet unidentified.

- [ ] Some organisms found in the Antarctic Ocean can withstand freezing temperatures because they naturally contain antifreeze in their blood.

- [ ] Many of the 'abyssal creatures', or species that inhabit the ocean below, have the ability to glow in the dark.

- [ ] A startling 25% of all marine species find a home on them, although they make up a very small portion of the ocean floor.

- [ ] Few of the most iconic prehistoric animals were the Dinosaur, Mammoth, Saber-toothed tiger, Pterodactyl, Megalodon etc.

Ant

- [ ] The ratio of ants to humans, on Earth, is 1:2.5 million. Being highly social creatures, ants may exist in colonies with up to 500,000 members.

☐ When an ant becomes drowsy, it always falls on its right side. Due to the structure of their jointed legs, ants have a somewhat larger right side. Their legs naturally bend when they move, which increases the likelihood that they will fall on their right side if they get sleepy or intoxicated.

☐ Ants usually do not like baby powder because it usually has talcum powder that acts as an ant repellent.

☐ Ants have no lungs. They lack a separate respiratory system from the lungs because they have an open circulatory system instead.

☐ The Egyptian queen (Cleopatra) added a faint shine and texture by using crushed ants as a base. Her lipstick had an eye-catching crimson color due to crushed beetles.

☐ Like many other living things, ants stretch their bodies as they wake up in the morning.

☐ Ants never rest or sleep. Their ability to store energy and use it gradually throughout the day is a result of their distinct physiology.

Axolotl

☐ One unique form of salamander that is the axolotl, which can regrow broken limbs and even the heart.

Bat

☐ You won't have to worry about bugs if you have a pet bat because they consume 3,000 insects every night.

☐ Bat scientists generally agree that when a bat exits a cave, it turns to the left. This has been explained by the fact that bats often follow echoes; hence, a mechanism to prevent collisions should be in place for them to escape.

☐ No bat can walk because their leg bones are too thin. Bats don't require strong leg bones to maintain their body weight, thus this adaptation is for flight.

Bear

☐ Koalas do not drink water. Being able to receive the essential fluids through eucalyptus leaves makes them one of the few animal species that can survive without drinking water.

☐ The true color of a polar bear's skin is black, not white. But because of the way it's transparent or clear fur reflects light and appears white; it is frequently described as having 'Issuer-like fur' because of how much it resembles snow and ice.

- [ ] All the polar bears seem left-handed. Since their noses are black and stand out against the dazzling white background, they use their right paw to conceal their noses as they approach their victim and their left paw to grasp it severely.

- [ ] The remarkable capacity of polar bears to hold their breath for extended periods is well recognized.

- [ ] There are 42 teeth in the mouths of bears, which are members of the Ursidae family. On the other hand, the average human mouth has 32 teeth.

- [ ] The oldest known stone tools that was discovered in Kenya dated to 3.3 million years ago.

- [ ] Depending on their nutrition and environment, black bears can exhibit a range of colors.

- [ ] Like kittens and puppies, bears are born with their eyes closed.

- [ ] Just out of curiosity, bears stand on their hind legs to smell accurately and view properly.

- [ ] Although the fur of polar bears appears white to us, however, it is transparent.

- [ ] Kodiak bears are the largest while the sun bears are the smallest bears in the world. Kodiak bears can stand 10 feet tall on their hind legs whereas the sun bears are usually 4–5 feet in length.

- [ ] The main food source for polar bears is fat, which when digested, produces water as a byproduct. They receive the fluids they need from this process to stay properly hydrated.

- [ ] Polar bears have a maximum swimming speed of 6.2 mph and a maximum swimming distance of 62 miles (100 km).

- [ ] The Polish brown bear named Wojtek was adopted by Polish soldiers in Iraq during World War II. In 1943, he entered the military and advanced swiftly to become a Corporal. Wojtek managed to carry out a variety of duties, such as carrying supplies and equipment.

- [ ] Together, the shorter undercoat and the longer outer coat of fur help to regulate body temperature and provide protection from water and ice. The polar bear is the one who has the thickest fur coat.

- [ ] Instead of being bears, koalas are marsupials that resemble kangaroos and wallabies and carry a pouch.

Bee

- [ ] Bees are able to identify faces in people.

- [ ] Even though there are about 20,000 different kinds of bees, less than 4% of them can generate honey.

- [ ] Bees have four wings and they can amazingly beat their wings almost 200 times each second.

- [ ] Bees kill more people as compared to snakes. The World Health Organization (WHO) estimates that allergic responses account for between 50,000 and 100,000 of the deaths caused by bee stings annually. On the other hand, 5,000–6,000 fatalities are caused by snakes annually.

- [ ] Honeybees may travel great distances at fifteen miles per hour to gather nectar and pollen for their hives. Their wings also beat at an amazing 200 times per second, which gives them the ability to fly, hover, and even produce lift.

- [ ] The eyes of honey bees are covered in hair. They can sense and navigate their environment with the aid of these hairs and other sensory organs.

- [ ] Bees are known to communicate through the 'waggle dance', in which they signal the existence of flowers that are rich in nectar.

- [ ] Bees can produce a potent venom that takes an amazing 22 muscles to sting.

Beetle

- [ ] Indeed, beetles are by far the most abundant and diverse collection of organisms on Earth. In actuality, beetles make up one in every four animals. Around 40% of all reported animal species are beetle species, with approximately 400,000 recognized species as of estimations.

- [ ] An object can be lifted by rhinoceros beetles 850 times their weight. To put this into perspective, a human being could move a 65-ton object if they had the strength of a rhinoceros beetle.

- [ ] Their bright colors or patterns on ladybugs act as a warning to prospective predators, letting them know that they are poisonous or have bad taste.

- [ ] For generations, the cochineal beetle has been a naturally occurring source of red pigment.

Bird

- ☐ Hummingbirds' nests are little, that resemble walnuts in size.

- ☐ Every day, baby robins consume 14 feet of earthworms or roughly 200 – 300 worms. This diet gives them the nutrition they need to thrive.

- ☐ Hummingbirds can fly backward. It is the only bird that can do so. They can fly in any direction due to the fast flapping of their wings.

- ☐ A hummingbird is not heavier than a penny. The smallest hummingbird, the Bee Hummingbird, weighs only 1.6 grams, which is remarkably less than the 2.5 – 5 grams of a penny.

- ☐ A flamingo can only consume food while its beak is twisted. The reason is that when its head is turned upside down, its uniquely shaped beaks and muscles enable it to filter small plants and animals from the water.

- ☐ Despite the large size of the deer, an eagle can kill it and fly away with it easily. The strong wings of the eagle make them able to do so.

- ☐ There is a huge parrot, Kea, which is native to New Zealand, is renowned for its intelligence. It is 2 feet long and has an odd appetite. It particularly enjoys pecking at and eating rubber materials, such as the strips that surround automobile windows.

- ☐ Owl's specific retina arrangement improves their dim light vision and makes them the only bird to see the color blue.

- ☐ It is thought that an eagle's vision is four to eight times more powerful than the ordinary human's.

- ☐ Many birds can sleep with one eye open because of this unusual adaptation, which keeps them alert.

- ☐ Some birds raise their lower eyelid when they blink, but owls only lower their upper eyelid.

- ☐ There are no eyeballs in Owl's eyes. Because of this, an owl can only see straight ahead and cannot 'roll' or move its eyes.

- ☐ The hummingbird is ten to fifteen times faster than other birds at batting its wings, with a maximum frequency of 200 beats per second.

- ☐ Like human naming customs, wild parrots have been known to give their offspring lifetime personal names.

- ☐ Its special ability allows Lyrebird to faithfully mimic nearly every sound, including mild sounds like camera shutters.

Bull

☐ Bulls typically move quicker uphill than downhill.

Cat

☐ A house cat normally has 18 claws in total.

☐ Dogs only have roughly ten vocal sounds, compared to more than one hundred in cats! Because cat whiskers are so sensitive, they might pick up even the smallest change in air current.

☐ There are 32 muscles in the cat's ear. Their ears can turn a complete 180 degrees because of this anatomical feature! This enables cats to orient their ears in the direction of distant and faint sounds to hear them more clearly, in addition to allowing them to express themselves through their ears.

☐ Particularly when exposed to ultraviolet light, cat urine shines quite brilliantly. Cats' urine contains phosphorus and the broken-down blood proteins glow in the dark.

☐ Cats are the only domestic animal that isn't mentioned in the Bible. The precise cause is unknown.

☐ A cat cannot move its jaw sideways and because of this phenomenon, it is unable to chew big food parts.

☐ Cats' whiskers enable cats to sense even the smallest variations in temperature and air pressure. To check if they can pass through a hole, they might use their whiskers.

☐ The only cat that is unable to retract its claws is the cheetah. A cat's front leg claws are entirely retractable because they must be sharp to grip prey, climb, or be used as a weapon in combat.

☐ In proportion to their body size, cats have the biggest eyes among all mammals. This feature helps them while stalking prey because their eyes are developed to pick up on even the smallest movements in their surroundings.

☐ Cats' sweat glands are located in their paws, lips, and chin and not all over their bodies. They use breathing and tearing to control their body temperature.

☐ Cats have three eyelids which keep their eyes clean and safe by this transparent lid, which is situated in the inner corner of the eye.

☐ Domestic cats can sleep for up to 16 hours a day on average.

- [ ] Sugar is not tasteable to cats. Cats lack the proteins that are essential to make the taste buds that identify sweetness. Overall, as compared to humans, cats have only a few hundred taste buds.

- [ ] There were two cats whose age was recorded as the oldest in the world. Their ages were 34 and 38 years. The owner of both was the same. She only gave her kitties coffee, veggies, bacon, and eggs. Despite the weirdness of this combination, it is obvious that their owner has found a recipe that has added to their extraordinary longevity.

- [ ] Blue eyes are unlucky for white cats. Stats show that 65% - 85% of the blue-eyed white cats are born deaf. On the other hand, the percentage of non-blue-eyed-deaf-white-cats lies between 17% - 22%.

Camel

- [ ] Camels have three eyelids instead of just one or two. The nictitating membrane, another name for the third eyelid, acts as a barrier to keep dust and sand out of their eyes.

- [ ] Hunting camels is prohibited in the state of Arizona. Camels kept by private owners, like those in zoos, circuses, or other tourist destinations, would already be covered by property rules.

- [ ] The Figure-Eight pattern is the eight-shaped pattern in which camels chew. Their mouth structure and tooth alignment are thought to be responsible for this unusual habit.

Chameleon

- [ ] The tongue of a chameleon is twice as long as its body, which allows them to catch the prey with supreme accuracy and helps them to survive.

- [ ] The eye movements of chameleons are entirely independent of one another. They have 360° vision and can look in nearly any direction.

Chicken

- [ ] The ratio of humans and chickens is almost 1:2. With 7.8 billion people on the planet, it is not unreasonable to assume that there are almost 20 billion chickens on the planet.

- [ ] Water is needed for poultry farming in large quantities—roughly 400 gallons. That is the equivalent of 6,400 glasses of water, to put things in context.

- [ ] Using over 30 different vocalizations, chickens can communicate with one another.

- ☐ Prolific backyard hens can produce as many as 250 eggs a year.

- ☐ Chickens cannot fly for long distances. However, the longest chicken flight ever recorded covered a distance of slightly over three hundred feet in 13 seconds.

Chimpanzee

- ☐ Humans share approximately 98.8% of their DNA with chimpanzees that makes it the closest-related species to humans.

- ☐ Chimpanzees are among the few non-human animals who can use tools for hunting and getting hunny.

Cow

- ☐ Listening to calming music increases the amount of milk that cows produce.

- ☐ Almost 200,000 cups of milk are produced by an average cow, during its entire life. It can yield 25 to 30 liters of milk on average per day, and the lactation period typically lasts 305 to 310 days.

- ☐ Research has repeatedly demonstrated that cows that are given names and personalized care typically yield higher milk yields.

- ☐ It's true that cows' size and physical makeup make them unfit for walking downstairs. On the other hand, they are efficient at moving uphill.

- ☐ Cows have hard thickened gum on their upper jaw instead of teeth. It is called a 'dental pad' and on their lower jaw, they have incisors that help to bite and grind the grass.

Cockroach

- ☐ Because of their special anatomy, cockroaches may survive for up to nine days without their heads. This is because cockroaches breathe through microscopic holes on their sides called spiracles.

- ☐ Fossilized cockroaches from 280 million years ago have been found.

Crocodile

- ☐ Crocodiles cannot extend their tongues. This is because their tongues are joined to the bottom of their mouths by a muscle strand.

- ☐ Alligators and crocodiles move very quickly on land. However, they can only go as fast as 9.5 miles per hour (15 kph) at their maximum speed, and they are not able to keep up that pace for very long.

- [ ] Alligators have been known to live much longer in captivity given the right care; some specimens have been known to live for up to 80–100 years.

- [ ] A crocodile's bite is 12 times more powerful than a great white sharks' bite.

- [ ] Like most other lizards, crocodiles can only get as big as their surroundings permit. It will never be able to expand beyond the physical confines of a small enclosure.

Dog

- [ ] The Chihuahua are just 5-9 inches tall and weigh only 2-6 pounds making them the smallest dog breed.

- [ ] During puberty, Chinese spotted dogs may get acne, just as people do. Hormonal changes are thought to be the main cause of acne in dogs.

- [ ] Certain dogs (without training) can detect when a person, usually a child, is about to experience an epileptic seizure.

- [ ] Every year, dogs and cats consume (pet food) worth more than $11 billion. This number demonstrates how important it is to provide pets with wholesome, satisfying meals.

- [ ] Just like humans, dogs and cats are either right- or left-handed (paws, indeed). It is proven by the tests conducted at the Institute for the Study of Animal Problems in Washington, D.C.

- [ ] Dogs do create hilarious noises, which are sometimes called 'play sneezes' or 'fake sneezes.'

- [ ] Just like a human fingerprint, a dog's nose print is unique and extraordinary.

- [ ] The Guinness World Record for the fastest dog-opened automobile window is held by Striker, a Border Collie, from Hungary. In just 11.34 seconds, Striker was able to wind down a car window that wasn't electronic.

- [ ] Zorba, an Old English Mastiff, was the largest dog according to Guinness World Records. It measured 8 feet 3 inches and weighed 343 pounds.

Dinosaur

- [ ] The word "Dinosaur" comes from the 2 Greek words *deinos* that means terrible and *sauros* that means lizard. So dinosaur can be translated as "terrible lizard."

- [ ] It is believed that dinosaurs roamed Earth for over 165 million years, which becomes even more fascinating when you consider that humans only appeared around five to seven million years ago.

- [ ] The experts believe that feathers or quill knobs were present on a large number of dinosaurs, including theropods and certain ceratopsians.

Donkey

- [ ] Approximately 1,000 people are killed by donkeys each year. A much lower number of fatalities brought on by plane crashes.

- [ ] A donkey can always see all its feet at once because its eyes are placed wide apart on its head.

- [ ] In quicksand, mules can stay floating because of their more compact and robust bodies. However, donkeys are more likely to sink.

- [ ] A zonkey is the hybrid child of a zebra and a pet donkey.

Duck

- [ ] The feathers of all ducks are extremely waterproof.

- [ ] Nobody knows why there is no echo of a duck's quack. The sound of a duck is unique and is a fading sound. So, maybe the actual sound and the echo are difficult to differentiate.

- [ ] Ducks have a distinctive walk with a distinctive head-bobbing motion.

- [ ] Ducks have better vision & can see colors that human cannot.

Elephant

- [ ] More than 5 liters of water can be stored in an elephant's trunk.

- [ ] Elephants can dive in water and swim for up to 6 hours.

- [ ] Elephants in the wild sleep for an average of only two hours every night, which makes them the least known snoozers of any mammal.

- [ ] African elephants have four long, curving incisors, sometimes referred to as tusks.

- [ ] The teeth of an adult elephant can weigh as much as nine pounds.

- [ ] An adult elephant needs 210 liters of water a day on average.

- [ ] Particularly elephants have been known to have a high degree of self-awareness; they have been seen to touch their own reflections.

- [ ] The skeleton of an elephant barely accounts for 15% of its overall weight.

- [ ] Elephants cannot pull themselves off the ground; they are just too heavy. Elephants weigh between 5,000 and 14,000 pounds, but they can run as fast as 16 miles per hour.

Fish

- [ ] The tongue of a blue whale weighs more than most elephants. The tongue of an adult blue whale can weigh anywhere from 5,000 to 6,000 pounds on average which is more than most of the elephants.

- [ ] Dolphins use a variety of sounds like clicking and whistling for communicating. In fact, every dolphin can produce a distinct sound.

- [ ] There is no brain in a starfish. They do, however, possess a distinct neural system that is dispersed throughout their body.

- [ ] Even when they are sleeping, sharks can't stop moving.

- [ ] Some fish species that live in deep oceans below 800 meters lack eyes. Because they do not need eyes to find food or identify predators at such depths due to the darkness and lack of light.

- [ ] Fish do not blink except for sharks. Thanks to the nictitating membrane that serves as an eyelid and distinguishes sharks from other fish.

- [ ] Certain animals, such as humpback whales, can go up to six months without eating.

- [ ] Humans have only 9,000 taste buds. The highest number of taste buds are present in catfish, which are located all over its body. The number of taste buds can reach up to 175,000 in some individuals.

- [ ] There is no brain in starfish. In reality, starfish lack both a brain and blood!

- [ ] A goldfish will ultimately turn white if kept in a dark place. The skin pigment of goldfish changes color in response to light. Their skin is affected when there is insufficient light exposure or deprivation.

- [ ] A jellyfish's body is 95% water. It is composed of only 5% being solid substance. When a jellyfish is submerged in water, it loses its intriguing qualities and becomes less of an attractive, enigmatic, and fascinating blob.

- [ ] Blue whale's heart is the biggest on the planet. It beats 9 times a minute and the heartbeat can be heard from a distance of 2 miles.

- [ ] Sharks have an acute sense of smell. They are able to identify a single drop of blood in 100 million parts of water.

- [ ] With each eye, dolphins may look in a different direction. With one eye open, they can snooze. Since only one hemisphere of the brain sleeps at a time, this kind of sleep is referred to as unihemispheric sleep.

- [ ] Small, V-shaped scales cover the shark's skin. By reducing drag, these denticles enable the shark to travel more swiftly and silently.

- [ ] Shark's teeth protrude out as they bite to seize the food. This is because the shark's body attempts to maximize its biting force to ensure that the feeding attempt is successful.

- [ ] At 50 miles per hour (81 km per hour), sailfish may leap from the water into the air. This amazing talent is probably an adaptation for attracting prey or interacting with other sailfish.

- [ ] A blue whale's maximum sound pressure is 188 decibels, the loudest sound a living being can make. It can be heard at a distance of up to 530 miles.

- [ ] Goldfish have a poor memory. However, research shows that goldfish are quick learners and can recall memories for one month.

- [ ] Jellyfish are also called immortal fish. This species biologically can undergo a process to change its body back into a younger one.

- [ ] The lifespan of a wildlife goldfish is 40 years. This is a significantly longer lifespan than the usual five to seven years for domesticated goldfish.

- [ ] Sharks lack bones, unlike humans and many other creatures, because they are cartilaginous fish.

- [ ] Sharks' teeth constantly grow throughout their lives. Some sharks like the bull sharks can have up to 50 rows of teeth, which they constantly shed and regenerate in their entire life.

- [ ] Certain shark species can produce light in the dark through internal chemical reactions.

- [ ] Sharks have eyelids; however, they do not blink. Rather, the main purpose of their eyelids is to shield their eyes from harm while they are attacked.

- [ ] Sharks are remarkably expert at picking up electrical impulses in the ocean.

- [ ] Electric eels can generate electricity up to 800 volts. More than 530 torch batteries would be needed to generate the same amount of electricity.

- [ ] Whale sharks lay the largest eggs, whether they are laid or not.

- [ ] The dolphin can react rapidly to possible dangers because half of its brain is in a deep sleep and the other half is awake and attentive.

- [ ] Sharks' corneas are successfully transplanted to humans, enabling vision restoration for patients.

- [ ] Sharks do engage in periods of rest throughout the day, but they are not completely sleeping.

- [ ] Because of its slow metabolism, the blue whale has the capacity for energy conservation.

- [ ] A blue whale typically weighs between 150 and 170 tonnes (136,000 and 152,000 lb). A whale can therefore weigh as much as thirty elephants!

- [ ] Indeed, dolphins are carnivores, meaning that meat is their main source of food.

- [ ] Dolphins use sounds such as clicking and whistling to communicate with one another.

- [ ] Jellyfish and lobsters have an endless lifespan as long as they don't get hurt, poisoned, or die from illness.

- [ ] With a rich evolutionary history spanning more than 400 million years, sharks are among the planet's oldest living animals.

- [ ] Most sharks have an average speed of up to 44 miles per hour.

- [ ] The 'ghost fish' is the deepest fish found, to date, thriving at 26,715 feet because of its amazing ability.

- [ ] Because wild salmon consume prawns, they are pink while farmed salmon don't eat prawns, their color is white.

- [ ] Fish of the garfish species are distinct due to their green-colored skeleton.

- [ ] Certain fish species can cough, especially those that have lungs or structures resembling lungs.

- [ ] Dolphins are exceptionally quick and nimble swimmers that have a top speed of 37 miles per hour.

- [ ] About 1,300 pounds in weight, the size of a blue whale's heart is so big that it is possible for a human to swim through its arteries.

- [ ] A single mouthful of krill can provide up to 457,000 calories for a blue whale.

☐ Goldfish can detect both ultraviolet (UV) and infrared (IR) light.

Flea

☐ A flea can jump 350 times its body length. It resembles a human being jumping a full football pitch.

☐ A flea can accelerate up to fifty times quicker than a space shuttle.

Butterfly

☐ The very toxic African Giant Swallowtail butterflies are so dangerous that they can kill up to six cats.

☐ If a butterfly's body temperature is below 86 degrees, it cannot fly. Because they are ectothermic, butterflies are incapable of controlling their body temperature.

☐ Butterflies come in a variety of sizes, from 1/8 inch to nearly 12 inches. Butterflies come in around 17,500 distinct species. The wings of butterflies are translucent. The true source of their color is the reflection of other colors via their wings.

☐ Many butterflies use their feet to sense whether a leaf they are sitting on is suitable for laying eggs that will eventually become food for their larvae.

☐ Butterflies come in roughly 24,000 different species. Even more abundant are the moths, of which 140,000 species have been identified worldwide.

☐ Butterflies and insects have exoskeletons, which means their bodies are covered with an external skeleton. In addition to keeping water inside their bodies to prevent them from drying out, an external skeleton protects the insect.

☐ Butterflies can see many colors that humans cannot. They can also see red, green, and yellow. This is a result of the distinct type of photoreceptor cell in their eyes.

☐ When the average life span of a butterfly is 2 – 4 weeks, the Brimstone butterfly wins the title of the longest-living butterfly by living up to nine to ten months.

☐ The butterflies passively absorb the salt by putting their proboscis in the turtles' tears.

☐ A butterfly's flying speed can be up to 12 miles per hour. Some moths have a 25-mph top speed! Skippers have been recorded to reach speeds of up to 37 mph, but the majority of butterflies simply glide along on their charming, mostly unpredictable flight patterns.

- ☐ Since moths lack stomachs, they mostly consume liquids like honey and nectar.

- ☐ Thanks to the microscopic sensors known as 'taste hairs' butterflies can taste with their feet. Their feet collect sensory data about the texture and flavor of the plant as they settle on it to feed or lay eggs.

- ☐ Butterflies consume their species and young ones. They may eat caterpillars, other butterflies, and even their eggs or pupae. This is called cannibalism.

Dragonfly

- ☐ With a top speed of 60 mph, dragonflies are undoubtedly some of the swiftest insects around. To add to their amazing flying ability is their quick flapping motion, which can occur up to 30–40 times per second.

- ☐ An average dragonfly lives for 6 months from egg to adult. However, if we see the life expectancy of only adults, it can be no more than a week or 2.

- ☐ With more than 28,000 separate lenses, several species of dragonflies can see their environment in remarkable detail.

Housefly

- ☐ Flies can't hear the sounds! They can't sense sound waves because they don't have ears.

- ☐ One of the main reasons houseflies might be difficult to swat is their reaction time, which is about 30 milliseconds.

- ☐ When flies take flight, they leap backwards. This is because they propel themselves into the air using their strong hind legs. Their wings beat quickly while they do this, creating lift and allowing them to move forward.

- ☐ A housefly will regurgitate and consume its food. As they don't have teeth and can't take a bite, they spray out an enzyme-rich saliva to consume it easily.

- ☐ Usually, a housefly flaps its wings 190 times in a second, and a human ear perceives that humming sound in the major scale of F. But this can change according to temperature and size.

- ☐ Surprisingly houseflies are abundant in protein, despite being pests. Studies on insects have shown that the protein content of a pound of houseflies can range from 60 to 70 grams more than that of a pound of beef.

Moth Fly

- ☐ Mammoths were prehistoric, large, elephant-like animal that lived during the Ice Age.
- ☐ Mammoths went extinct about 4,000 years ago.
- ☐ Mammoth remains like fossils and frozen specimens were found in Siberia, Europe, North America and Asia.

Moth Fly

- ☐ Some moth species have females that don't fly but crawl because they have no wings. Females that exhibit this behavior are known as aptery.

- ☐ The typical garden type caterpillar has 248 muscles in its skull. Caterpillars can move their numerous body segments and modify their mouth parts for eating because they have a large number of muscles.

- ☐ Adult moths lack a mouth that's why they never ingest anything. Their only source is the stored energy while they were caterpillars.

- ☐ Certain species of Snout Moths (Pyralididae) have caterpillars that reside in or on water plants. These caterpillars are an essential component of wetland ecosystems because of their remarkable adaptation, which enables them to flourish in aquatic settings.

- ☐ A few moth caterpillars (Psychidae) construct a protective shell (made up of from silk and soil or plant fragments) around themselves that they carry with them at all times.

Fox

- ☐ Fox naturally senses the Earth's magnetic field, which helps them to calculate distances. It is believed that they have evolved this special ability to help them with hunting and navigation.

Frog

- ☐ The distinctive croaking sounds are usually only made by male toads.

- ☐ Frogs have the unique ability to live even after being frozen. Because of their special adaptation, they can survive in places where others might not make it through the hard winters.

- ☐ As amphibians, frogs have a special method of absorbing nutrients and water through their skin.

- ☐ Given their body size, which makes it challenging for their brain to regulate swallowing while maintaining an open eye.

☐ A frog's ability to regurgitate was discovered during a space trip. The frog opens its jaws and lets its stomach hang out before it vomits. After completely emptying the stomach with its forearms, the frog swallows the stomach back down.

Giraffe

☐ With the help of 21-inch-long tongue, giraffes can easily clean their ears. This extraordinary talent helps them keep their ears free of debris and parasites that could enter the ear canal.

☐ The ability to survive without water is more in rats and giraffes than in camels. Giraffes may live for three weeks whereas rats can live their whole lives without drinking water! However, a camel can survive for up to 15 days without water.

☐ Did you know that the necks of giraffes and humans contain the same number of bones?

☐ Although giraffes are not natural swimmers, they can swim (badly) if needed.

Gorilla

☐ The average gorilla sleeps for 14 hours per day.

☐ We humans share around 98% of our DNA with gorillas.

Hippopotamus

☐ A hippopotamus's mouth can expand to 180 degrees; therefore, a child standing four feet tall might fit within.

☐ Hippos close their ears while submerged in water. They can sense vibrations in the water through their jaw bones.

☐ It is true that hippos, or hippopotamuses, are born underwater.

Horse

☐ The horse's only means of breathing is through their noses.

☐ Unlike people, cows and horses are big ruminants, so they cannot lie down to sleep as humans can.

☐ You can tell how old a horse is by looking at their teeth.

Hedgehog

☐ A hedgehog's heart beats around 300 times each minute on average much like a drum line of their own.

Iguana

☐ An iguana can hold its breath underwater for up to 28 minutes, which gives them the ability to hide from predators or surprise their prey.

Insect

☐ Your feet have a higher concentration of bacteria making them more susceptible to bug bites.

☐ Because a grasshopper's blood doesn't have red blood cells, it appears white or clear.

☐ Insects outnumber humans by 100,000,000 to 1. They are therefore abundant on Earth.

☐ It's critical to be aware that problems with lice can occur, particularly in communal spaces like schools.

☐ Some insects, like water striders and water walkers, have the unusual capacity to sit and even walk on the water's surface.

☐ Most insect blood contains specific colors like yellow or green.

☐ Many insects make a buzzing sound. It is because of the way their wings are built and function.

☐ In the world, there are about 200 million insects for every human.

Kangaroo

☐ Kangaroos mostly depend on their tails for stability and balance.

☐ Kangaroos and emus are unable to walk backward. Kangaroos are renowned for their amazing jumping skills, whereas emus are often fast-moving creatures with strong legs but not for reverse walking!

☐ Kangaroos are tiny at birth, roughly the size of a grape or small pea that could fit in a teaspoon.

Lion

☐ A lion's roar is so loud that it can be heard five miles away. Lions use their loud and long-range roars to alert other lions to their existence and warn possible enemies to avoid them.

☐ After a full moon, lions are more inclined to attack at night. While it is true that lions hunt at night, their habits are more influenced by social dynamics than by lunar cycles.

- [ ] A wild lion typically makes between 5 to 20 kills in a year, with an average of around 10-15 kills per annum.

- [ ] A lion's roar can carry up to five miles and even warn others of approaching danger.

Lizard

- [ ] The horned lizard's well-known feature is its ability to expel blood from its eyes to scare the predators, which helps it to escape!

- [ ] A lizard's ability to self-amputate its tail provides it safety. However, it grows again in a few months. This is frequently done as a defensive tactic to divert predators.

Mole

- [ ] In just one night, a mole can dig a 300-foot-long tunnel. Their strong body, keen claws, and strong front legs enable them to succeed in this feat.

Monkey

- [ ] Monkeys went to space even long before humans did so. On June 14, 1949, a monkey named Albert II was sent to the space successfully for the first time.

- [ ] Certain monkey species can age into baldness or hair loss, just as humans.

Mosquito

- [ ] Mosquitoes that bite are only females because female mosquitoes require a blood meal to lay eggs.

- [ ] Carbon dioxide (CO_2) released by people and other animals attracts mosquitoes.

- [ ] People are exclusively bitten by female mosquitoes as they need blood as food to lay eggs.

Octopus

- [ ] The brain of an octopus is located in its tentacles. For a brief while after being detached from the body, the tentacles still look for food and eventually carry it to a mouth that is no longer there.

- [ ] An octopus must be brilliant due to its vast nerve network as they have nine brains.

- [ ] Octopuses indeed have three hearts, which is an important adaptation to their unusual body configuration.

Ostrich

☐ The eye of an ostrich is larger than its brain. It measures 5 cm across which is the biggest eye among all terrestrial mammals.

☐ A myth, that ostriches bury their heads in sand when they sense danger, was proven wrong by observing 200,000 ostriches for 80 years. Not a single ostrich stuck its head under the sand.

☐ The brain of an ostrich comprises only one-third of the entire skull volume of the bird. On the other hand, its eyes are the biggest of any bird.

☐ Ostriches frequently lie flat on the ground when they feel frightened or alarmed.

☐ A quick horse can go 30 and 40 mph on a longer run, but the ostrich can continuously maintain speeds of 45 mph.

Panda

☐ Baby pandas are roughly the size of a mouse and can weigh as low as 1/4 pound (100 grams).

Penguin

☐ Penguins' eyes contain a system that converts salt water to fresh water.

☐ The emperor penguin, can remain underwater for up to 27 minutes.

☐ The only birds that can't fly but swim are penguins. It can move quickly and with remarkable ability through the water.

☐ Penguins can't fly but they can jump up to six feet into the air.

☐ In 2009, snipers were deployed to Australia to protect a penguin colony from potential threats to ensure the survival of this endangered species.

☐ To present as gifts to their loved ones, penguins look for particular pebbles.

☐ Penguins are well-known for their long-lasting pair relationships.

☐ There is a special organ that penguins have that helps them filter out excess salt from the water they drink.

☐ Penguins can stay underwater for extended periods. Certain kinds of penguins have been known to submerge for as long as 27 minutes.

Rabbit

☐ Rabbits' special eye anatomy allows them to see in all directions.

☐ Doe, buck, and kit are the names for female, male, and baby rabbits, respectively.

Reindeer

☐ Because of its hollow structure, reindeer hair—also referred to as caribou hair—is very unique.

Rhinoceros

☐ Rhino horns are entirely formed of keratin, a naturally occurring protein, in contrast to the majority of animal horns, which are composed of a bony core covered in a comparatively thin layer of keratin.

Rodent

☐ Up to 200 trees can be consumed by a single beaver annually.

☐ Rats grow so fast that they can multiply from 2 to over a million in just 18 months. Rats only live for two to three years on average in the wild.

☐ Rats and horses are among those animals that can't throw up. Due to their physiology and anatomy, they are unable to do so.

☐ Rodents keep grinding their teeth to keep them sharp and trimmed because rodent's teeth keep growing throughout their lives.

☐ Science claims that when rats are tickled, they do indeed react with laughter. Their laughter is inaudible to human ears.

☐ An average porcupine has 30,000 sharp spines (quills) on its body to protect its body from predators.

☐ A solitary beaver chops down up to 200 trees a year to create and maintain their lodges, which are their dwellings.

Scorpio

☐ Scorpions sting themselves, and they would die if a small amount of alcohol is applied to them.

☐ Scorpios are extremely strong animals that can live without food for as long as a year.

Shrimp

☐ The heart of a shrimp is located on the thorax, just behind its head.

☐ In the early stages, a lobster would typically gain 0.04 ounces (1 gram) of weight per month. It takes an amazing seven years to reach one pound which is the equivalent of 84 months or 2,592 days of consistent growth.

☐ Hemagenin bonds to lobster blood when it comes into contact with oxygen, giving the fluid the color blue.

Sea lion

☐ The capacity of sea lions to generate rhythmic noises, including the ability to clap in time with a beat.

Skunk

☐ The powerful smell of a skunk is known for its extraordinary range. Humans can sense the distinctive smell up to one mile (1.6 kilometres) away.

Slug

☐ Slugs have a strong sense of smell. They have four noses to sense different types of smells.

Snail

☐ Snails can't live in dry and hot weather. Their bodies create mucus to shield them from the weather and for up to three years they can sleep in this state.

☐ The radula, a special part of a snail's mouth, has over 25,000 tiny teeth. Due to these, snails can effectively scrape and grind plant materials.

☐ The mean velocity of a garden snail is approximately 0.05 km/h (0.03 mi/h). That moves very slowly!

Snake

☐ With a maximum length of approximately thirty feet, the reticulated python is the longest snake in the world.

☐ Even though common cobra venom is 40 times more poisonous than cyanide, it does not rank among the top ten venoms.

☐ The Australian Brown Snake's venom is so potent, that a human can be killed by just 1/14,000th of an ounce.

☐ Conjoined snakes have two heads. These two heads fight with each other for food.

☐ A wide variety of non-venomous snakes are found in the northeastern state of Maine.

☐ Snakes are pure carnivores, which means that their only source of nourishment is animal flesh.

- Three kinds of venomous snakes can be found on the Australian island of Tasmania: the Tiger, Copperhead, and Swamp snakes. Each of the three species is deadly poisonous.

- A snake that tries to bite someone when it's in a river or marsh will find it difficult to breathe and may even drown from lack of oxygen.

- Even with their eyelids closed, the majority of snakes have a specialized sense of heat and movement.

- Pythons have the unusual capacity to sense heat thanks to specific pits on their snouts called thermoreceptive organs.

Spider

- A spider's web serves as a trap for food rather than a home. Every web design is different. There are tropical spiders that can weave webs up to eighteen feet in diameter.

- Surveys show that the majority of people fear spiders more than death. Surprisingly, fewer people fear Champagne corks despite the fact that they are more likely to kill you than spiders.

- The black widow is the most poisonous spider. Although the venom of black widows is fifteen times more deadly than that of rattlesnakes, humans are rarely killed by it.

- It is possible for tarantulas to live for up to two years without eating.

- Hemolymph, the term for spider blood, is transparent, much like water.

Squid

- The world's largest eye award goes to the giant squid. It measures 10 inches in diameter; which is the same as the size of a human skull or a dining plate.

- 8 arms and 2 larger tentacles make up the standard 10 appendages of a large squid.

Squirrel

- Squirrels can warn one another of impending danger, the approach of a predator, or even just a rival squirrel by twitching their tails.

- The lifespan of a squirrel varies from 2 to 9 years, contingent upon species, habitat, and food supply.

☐ Although squirrels can live up to nine years, several factors affect how long they survive.

Termite

☐ Termites collectively weigh more than humans on this earth. For each person, there are 1,000 pounds of termites.

☐ When heavy metal music is played, it is observed that termites consume food twice as quickly.

Tiger

☐ Like the tiger's fur, its skin is also striped. Their skin coloring, which is influenced by their DNA, includes the stripes.

☐ Despite their reputation for being wary and possessive, tigers have been successfully trained to use litter boxes by certain professionals.

Turtle

☐ Sea turtles use Earth's magnetic field, to go to the same beach where they were born, and lay eggs.

Wolf

☐ It is true that wolves are the only ancestors of all domestic dog breeds.

☐ The name 'wild dog' refers to a wider range of animals, such as coyotes, dingoes, and wolves, all of which are separate species but have an ancestral connection.

Worm

☐ There is a phenomenon known as 'autophagy', in which some invertebrates—including worms—consume their bodies to survive when they don't find food.

AIRPLANES AND AIRPORTS

☐ According to aviation experts, every commercial plane experiences a lightning strike at least once a year. However, passengers don't recognize, when!

☐ The black box in the airplane is not black but bright orange in color to be recognized easily in the event of a crash.

☐ Commercial airplanes are deliberately painted white to reflect maximum sunlight, keep the plane cooler, and prevent the airplane from damaging solar radiation.

☐ You can get oxygen only for 12 – 15 minutes from the automatically drop-down oxygen masks in the airplane.

☐ The passengers sitting in the back seats of an airplane are 40% safer than the ones sitting in the front rows.

☐ Even if an engine malfunctions or fails, a commercial airplane can fly for several hours with a single engine.

☐ Based on passenger numbers, Hartsfield–Jackson Atlanta International Airport in Atlanta, Georgia, is the busiest airport in the world.

- [ ] Airplane tires are so strong that they can be used 500 times, withstand multiple landings and taking-offs, carry weight for up to 38 tons, and withstand speeds of up to 170mph.

- [ ] The world's longest non-connecting commercial flight is operated by Singapore Airlines. It flies from Singapore to New York for 19 hours and covers almost 9,500 miles.

- [ ] By eliminating an olive from first-class salads in 1987, American Airlines was able to save $40,000 without affecting the experience of the passengers. Today, after accounting for inflation, this would equate to a savings of about $100,000 per year.

- [ ] In 2014, a Chinese enjoyed free food at the airport's VIP lounge for almost a year. He purchased China Eastern Airlines' first-class ticket and canceled and rebooked it 300 times. Once the airline detected his scam, he canceled his ticket for a refund.

- [ ] There are no airports inside the borders of five nations: Vatican City, San Marino, Liechtenstein, Andorra, and Monaco.

- [ ] 56% of pilots on British airlines acknowledge that they have slept off while flying, and 29% report waking up to find their co-pilot slept out.

- [ ] The largest airplane in the world is Antonov's An-225 Mriya. It is 250 feet long with a 290-foot wingspan. It can carry up to 640 tons of cargo!

- [ ] In 2003, Boeing 727 was stolen by two unknown persons from Luanda, Angola. Neither the jet nor the thieves have ever been found.

- [ ] The world's smallest commercial flight, which is only 1.7 miles long and can be completed in 47 seconds, is between the two tiny Orkney Islands in Scotland's north.

- [ ] A local specialty, pesto sauce, is an exception at Genoa's airport because the sauce has cultural value in the area. Their pesto scanner is unique.

- [ ] In the 1930s, airports were required to standardize their names with airport codes; hence, those having two-letter names merely appended an 'x', resulting in names like LAX.

- [ ] At 78.2 degrees north latitude, Svalbard Airport, Longyear, located in Svalbard, Norway, is the world's northernmost airport with regular flights.

- [ ] The world's southernmost airport is Malvinas Argentina's International Airport in Ushuaia, Argentina, at 54.8 degrees south latitude.

ARTS & ENTERTAINMENT

☐ In the whole world, the most-sung song is 'Happy Birthday to You'.

☐ Viewers from all over the world spend more than 1 billion hours watching YouTube content daily.

☐ 'Think' is the motto of IBM. Afterwards, Apple adopted its tagline 'Think different'.

☐ Vincent Van Gogh, in his life, sold only one painting, 'Red Vineyard at Arles'. Sadly, he spent his whole life in struggle and poverty.

☐ Every year, India produces 800 films whereas 500 films are made by the US per annum.

☐ The time shown on a watch in the majority of watch advertising is 10:10. This time resembles a smile. Secondly, the brand name and logo are visible at 10:10.

☐ In the movie 'Pulp Fiction' all the clocks are stuck at 4:20. This oddity has grown to be recognized as a defining feature of the movie.

☐ Almost 5,000 ads are displayed in America every day. Whereas, the number of online viewed ads, globally, is almost 5.3 trillion per annum.

☐ Walt Disney's Mickey Mouse was originally known as Mortimer but his wife suggested Mickey. This character became so famous that in 1933, it got 800,000 fan letters.

☐ An ancient flute was found in a cave that was thought to be 60,000 years old. Amazingly it is still in working condition.

☐ With more than 33 seasons and 700 episodes shown to date, The Simpsons is the longest-running primetime scripted program in television history.

☐ Beethoven, a renowned composer, often dipped his head in cold water before composing the legendary compositions.

☐ A typical person watches approximately 5,600 films in their lifetime, according to some estimates. This equates to approximately 2.5 films every day or 12 films every week.

☐ The television program that has aired the most episodes is 'The Simpsons'.

☐ Based on the information gathered, Nollywood in Nigeria produces around 2,000 films annually, more than Hollywood and Bollywood combined.

- [ ] Walt Disney himself debated between naming Mickey Mouse and Mortimer, the cartoon character.

- [ ] Toto was an iconic character played by Terry in the 1939 picture 'Wizard of Oz'. She was paid 125$ per week at that time, which is equal to $2729 today.

- [ ] The word DREAMS is created when the first letters of the main characters of the movie Inception are combined which are Dom, Robert, Eames, Arthur, Mal, and Saito.

- [ ] Shark attacks off the coast of the Jersey Shore are the phenomenon that served as the basis for the film Jaws. Five verified attacks on the coasts of New Jersey and New York took place in July 1916; three people were injured and five people died as a result.

- [ ] Throughout their lives, a lot of exceptionally talented individuals struggle to be recognized, frequently as a result of a lack of resources and networking opportunities. An artist's genuine worth is awarded to them after their passing.

- [ ] Walt Disney established a distinct code for his male staff members that prohibited men from sporting beards or mustaches.

- [ ] It's true that one of the earliest toys to be promoted on television was Mr. Potato Head.

ASTRONOMY

- [ ] The rare event of a February without a full moon occurs after every 19 years. The last such celestial event happened in 1999.

- [ ] Tears normally fall down your cheeks when you cry. But in space, they form bubbles around your eyes because of zero gravity.

- [ ] Birds require gravity to eat, therefore if NASA launched them into space, they would die quickly.

- [ ] Earth does not have a ring system. It might have been present in the past.

- [ ] The moon is moving away from the Earth slowly and constantly. It moves away a little but measurable distance per annum.

- [ ] The amazing blue sunset phenomenon that occurs on Mars! This occurs due to the unusual atmospheric conditions of the Red Planet.

- [ ] The massive celestial body Antares, a star, is 60,000 times bigger than our sun.

- [ ] The term 'Planet X', often known as 'Planet Nine', describes a possible planet that has not yet been found in our solar system.

- [ ] Jupiter, the fifth planet in the solar system, is the largest planet. If all the planets of the solar system are combined, they will make less than half of the Jupiter's mass.

- [ ] In space, it is completely silent. In other words, space is a vacuum because the density of air particles is so low there.

- [ ] It would take you less than an hour to reach space if you could drive a car straight up.

- [ ] Astronomers have discovered a planet orbiting another star, and they think the planet is mostly made of diamonds.

- [ ] An estimated 25 million pieces of debris enters the Earth's atmosphere per day.

- [ ] The age of our solar system is estimated to be 4.5 billion years.

- [ ] Every year, more than 500 meteorites weighing more than 10 pounds (4.5 kilogrammes) make it to Earth.

- [ ] Our Milky Way galaxy revolves around an enormous black hole whose mass is equal to 4 million suns.

- [ ] The odd smell of space has been likened by astronauts to a combination of rum, charred steak, and raspberries.

- [ ] Pen performance is impacted by the absence of gravity and air resistance in space.

- [ ] Halley's Comet was first observed by the Chinese in 240 BC, making it one of the comet's earliest known sightings.

- [ ] In 2015, the first crop grown in space by astronauts was red romaine lettuce.

- [ ] An Olympic-sized swimming pool has a capacity of around 660,430 liters and a grain of salt has a volume of approximately 0.06 milliliters. If we refer to the milky way stars as salt grains, it is possible that all the stars would completely fill an Olympic-sized swimming pool.

- [ ] According to scientific theory, carbon is crushed into diamonds in highly hot and dense settings like those on Jupiter and Saturn due to extreme pressure.

- [ ] The Sun, with its about 1.4 million km diameter might hold more than a million Earths, to put its vastness into perspective.

☐ Every year, an average of 100 people choke to death while using ballpoint pens.

☐ The number 57 on the Heinz ketchup container stands for the variety of pickles the firm used to offer. Even though the firm later discontinued many of those types.

☐ Among the youngest sons of the youngest son, Benjamin Franklin was the fifth in a series.

☐ Every day, 12 babies are handed to the wrong parents on average. But luckily most of these errors are identified and corrected before the infants leave the hospital.

☐ The fear of open spaces (Kenophobia) is more common in people than the fear of closed spaces (claustrophobia).

☐ 9 million people in the world share the same birthday as yours.

☐ There haven't been any new animals domesticated in the past 4,000 years.

☐ The left foot was put on the moon by Neil Armstrong when he reached there.

☐ Wasps taste like pine nuts. Moreover, insects have distinct flavors. For example, worms taste like fried bacon, and beetles like apples.

☐ Charles Osborne got the longest attack of hiccups, which lasted for 68 years. He holds the Guinness World Record for his longest suffering.

☐ It is true that yelling can transform its sound energy into measurable heat. The calculations show that if you yelled continuously for 8 years, 7 months, and 6 days, the energy would be sufficient to heat a cup of coffee.

☐ Recent data indicates that every year in the United States, about 2,700 individuals are released from hospitals with surgical items left inside of them. Regretfully, these surgical errors directly resulted in the deaths of 57 patients in 2000.

☐ A British gymnast fell from a fourth-floor window but luckily escaped death by performing a somersault and landing on his feet.

☐ A ten-year-old mattress weighs twice as much as it did when it was brand-new due to debris that accumulates over time. Dust mites, millions of dead skin cells, dandruff, soil, sand, and a lot of sweat are among the debris.

- [ ] Fishing is the most dangerous occupation in the United States. One in every 900 people passes away while at work.

- [ ] A person with a rare neurological condition known as Foreign Accent Syndrome (FAS) may often talk in his mother tongue with a foreign accent.

- [ ] Carrots improve one's night vision - this idea first appeared during World War II. Radar and thermal imaging were employed in British night vision technology, which the German military feared. Therefore, they spread the false myth that British soldiers were consuming a lot of carrots in order to improve their night vision.

- [ ] A person typically laughs 15 times a day.

- [ ] The only number where the quantity of letters required to write it equals its numerical value is four.

- [ ] The people we see in our dreams are those with whom we have had experiences in the past, including close friends, family, and even lovers.

- [ ] It can take 60 to 120 drops, depending on the liquid's viscosity, to fill a teaspoon.

- [ ] Hand washing dirty dishes in a day uses 27 gallons of water. However, an effective dishwasher minimizes water usage by up to 4 to 5 gallons.

- [ ] November babies may have a higher risk of becoming serial killers.

- [ ] Calendars and international organizations do not recognize February 30th as a date, and it does not exist in the modern era.

- [ ] People called it 'hypnopompic awakening' and often wake up at about 3:44 AM.

- [ ] Your immune system can be weakened for up to four or five hours if you become irritated for just a minute.

- [ ] For little creatures such as chipmunks and hummingbirds, time appears to slow down because of a phenomenon known as 'dilated time'.

- [ ] Light from stars and other celestial bodies takes time to get to us. Put otherwise, the light we perceive has already passed.

- [ ] The day of April 11, 1954, is considered 'Black Thursday' or 'The Day Nothing Happened'.

- [ ] The old English time system gave rise to the idea that a moment lasts approximately 1 minute and 30 seconds.

- Many people believe that 7 a.m. is the most typical time for humans to wake up.

- The amazing story of Terry Wallis, who in 1984 to 2021 spent an incredible 37 years in a coma.

- Due to the recycling process, in an average home, almost thirty percent of the indoor water comes from the toilet.

- It is discovered that an individual weighing about 154 pounds possesses about 0.2 milligrams of gold.

- People have been eating insects for ages in North, Central, and South America, Africa, Australia, Asia, and the Middle East because a lot of bugs are rich in protein and a good source of lipids, vitamins, and minerals. This practice is called 'Entomophagy'.

- The statement that was printed on US gold coins once was 'In Gold We Trust'.

- Nearly 61,000 people are flying over the United States at any given time. The United States alone accounts for about 29,000 daily flights.

- President John F. Kennedy could read ten times faster than a normal human. He could read four newspapers in 20 minutes.

- If you see the statue of a person in a park with both front legs raised, it means that the person died in combat. If the horse only has one front leg raised, it indicates that the person died from wounds sustained in combat; and if the horse has all four legs on the ground, it indicates that the person died from natural causes.

- There are 87,000 Americans on the transplant waiting list, which means that a sizable number of lives depend on the availability of organs.

- The majority of the people you see in your dreams are people you have met at some point in your life, even if only briefly. So, you can't dream of strangers.

BOOKS, COMIC BOOKS & WRITERS

☐ Marvel Comics created a character – Blue Ear, who was wearing a special hearing aid. This character was specially made for a four-year-old Anthony Smith who refused to wear his hearing aid because superheroes don't wear them.

☐ In his debut appearance in 1962, the character Hulk was gray. However, later, it was changed to green to overcome the printing glitches with the color gray.

☐ As of 2023, Bob Bretall, a US citizen, holds the record for having the world's largest comic book collection, with more than138,000 comic books.

☐ In April 2024, the purchase of Action Comic #1, for $6 million, made it the most expensive comic book ever sold.

☐ In 1755, the world's first English dictionary was composed.

☐ Chess was the subject of the first book printed in England.

☐ The name Wendy had never been recorded before the Peter Pan novel.

☐ The book that has the longest title, of 3,777 words, is 'The Historical Development of the Heart...' by Yethindra Vityala.

☐ The book that is most frequently stolen from libraries is the Guinness Book of Records. The book is famous for being a thief's target because of its accessibility and popularity.

☐ The first novel written by using a typewriter was 'The Adventures of Tom Sawyer'.

☐ Shakespeare is attributed to create and use more than 1,000 new words in his writings, which are still in use.

☐ Julius Caeser's autograph would value about $2,000,000, according to an estimation.

☐ Almost 5-7 billion copies of the Bible have been sold worldwide making it the world's consistently best-selling book. Ironically, because of its widespread appeal, it is also the most commonly stolen book from shops.

☐ The story 'Tales of 1001 Arabian Nights originally started from, 'Aladdin was a little Chinese boy'.

- [ ] Before World War II, the NY phone book had 22 Hitlers. But after World War II, there was no Hitler in the New York phone directory.

- [ ] Renowned German writer, Johann Wolfgang von Goethe could only write when he had an apple decaying in his desk drawer and he could not bear the sound of barking dogs.

- [ ] Mountain Magazine, the UK's best-selling hiking publication, has come under fire for releasing the wrong route for Ben Nevis, the highest peak in Scotland.

- [ ] In the 1960s, Finnish communists attempted to prohibit Donald Duck from Finland, only because he lacked pants.

- [ ] The famed Harry Potter author J.K. Rowling made history by becoming one of the wealthiest persons on the planet by selling books.

- [ ] 'A Dictionary of the English Language' by Samuel Johnson was released in 1755.

- [ ] There were just 50 listings in the first telephone book, popularly referred to as the 'New Haven Directory', which was released in 1878.

BUILDINGS & MASSIVE MONUMENTS

☐ The Florida theme park Disney World is larger than almost 17 nations worldwide.

☐ The Bahamas formerly had an underwater postal service. When it was first opened in 1996, it was a one-of-a-kind attraction.

☐ The clock comes to mind when we think of Big Ben in London. It's actually the bell. The large bell weighs more than 13 tons.

☐ Over 130 years before the construction of Sagrada Familia in Barcelona was started, it is still unfinished.

☐ You can keep yourself updated with the time by following Big Ben's Twitter account. It tweets hourly with the corresponding number of 'Bong'.

☐ A roadway passes through, between the fifth and seventh floors of the Abenobashi Terminal Building, which is situated in Osaka, Japan.

☐ The stately home of the British king, Buckingham Palace, is a magnificent building with an astounding 602 rooms. In addition to 188 staff bedrooms, 52 royal and staff bedrooms, 92 staterooms, and countless magnificent halls, hallways, and staircases

☐ The 1,792 steps of the Eiffel Tower are quite the workout, aren't they? To stop Nazi officials, such as Hitler, from utilizing the lift to swiftly climb the tower, French resistance fighters cut the lift cables in 1940.

☐ It's interesting to note that the Empire State Building's outside is adorned with over 10 million bricks, while its main structural components are made of steel and concrete.

☐ In Sweden (Jukkasjärvi village), there's a hotel made completely of ice. It is rebuilt every year using about five thousand tons of ice taken from the neighboring Torne River.

☐ The Pentagon in is a multi-winged structure with 5 concentric rings. The building possesses a 5-acre central courtyard and 5 floors.

☐ Did you know that the main library at Indiana University has an extensive collection of books, but the building's foundation couldn't support the book's weight and is sinking an inch annually.

☐ The Hoover Dam was constructed in 1936. It is claimed that it will last for two millennia (2000 years). The massive concrete used for the building is still hardening. It's predicted that the concrete will take another 500 years to cure to its maximum degree.

- ☐ The oldest and biggest zoo in the world is the Zoological Garden in Berlin. It has more than 1,500 animal species and more than 1,700 animals from all over the world.

- ☐ The total estimated length of the wire ropes holding the Golden Gate Bridge is 80,000 feet, which is sufficient to go around the Earth three times!

- ☐ The Golden Gate Bridge needs regular maintenance. As soon as the painting is done, the seawater starts corroding the paint and the bridge needs to be repainted immediately.

- ☐ Disneyland, not the Louvre or the Eiffel Tower, is the most visited tourist attraction in Paris.

- ☐ The Statue of Liberty has 25-foot-long feet. By taking her foot size into account, her shoe size is 879.

- ☐ Based on historical accounts, the construction of this huge pyramid took approximately 23 years, and involved the use of 2.3 million stone blocks, each weighing approximately 2.5 tonnes.

- ☐ From space, one can view China's Great Wall. It's a widely held myth!

- ☐ The Eiffel Tower, which is primarily composed of iron, rises up to six inches as a result of the metal expanding when it absorbs heat.

- ☐ According to archaeological estimates, Stonehenge actually dates to the late Neolithic era, about 5,000 years ago.

- ☐ Erected in Agra, India, between 1632 and 1653, the Taj Mahal is one of the earliest specimens of Mughal architecture.

- ☐ The tallest state capitol in the union is located in Louisiana, at 460 feet, it has 34 stories.

- ☐ The Pontiac Silverdome is the biggest NFL stadium that can accommodate almost 80,600 football fans.

- ☐ In New York City, Columbia University owns the second-largest land after the Catholic Church. The vast property holdings of Columbia University are put to use for academic buildings, research facilities, and other campus structures.

- ☐ One ton of cement is poured annually for every man, woman, and child.

- [ ] Bruce Lee's action moves were so fast that the director had to play the film in slo-mo to see his moves.

- [ ] In a competition to find a Charlie Chaplin look-alike, Charlie Chaplin himself once took third place.

- [ ] There is an iconic phrase attributed to Sherlock Holmes, that is, 'Elementary, my dear Watson'. However, this phrase is nowhere to be found in his texts.

- [ ] Psychoanalysis's creator and Austrian neurologist, Sigmund Freud was afraid of ferns.

- [ ] The first airplane fatality was a Frenchman Thomas Selfridge. Orville Wright was also on the flight and got seriously injured.

- [ ] The legendary British band Duran Duran found inspiration in the 'Durand-Durand' character of Jane Fonda picture 'Barbarella', released in 1968 and chose their name as Duran Duran.

- [ ] Einstein had trouble speaking until he was nine years old. At first, his parents even thought that he might be mentally handicapped.

- [ ] After the assassination of Abraham Lincoln, his dog Fido was also killed.

- [ ] David Bowie claimed that he had seen a person in a huge pink bunny costume several times, at many performances. However, he got worried when he saw the pink bunny in the same flight as soon as he entered the plane.

- [ ] James Cameron got so much inspiration from the movie Star Wars that he gave up his job as a truck driver and started his career as a filmmaker.

- [ ] According to James Cameron, the idea for the Terminator came from a disturbing nightmare in which a future robot broke into his hospital room and tried to kill him.

- [ ] Mr. Universe of the year 1952 was Monhar Aich. Now he is 100+ but still fit and active and goes to the gym regularly.

- [ ] Mahatma Gandhi never got the Nobel Peace Prize despite being nominated 5 times.

- [ ] The voice of Winnie Pooh, Jim Cummings, talks to very ill hospitalized children in Pooh voice, on call, to make them smile.

- [ ] Adolf Hitler is an unusual recipient of the Nobel Peace Prize given his savage deeds. Thus, he was nominated for it!

- [ ] An individual's record of earning the most Academy Awards is held by Walt Disney. Throughout his career, he has won 26 Oscar Awards out of 63 nominations.

- [ ] Famed Italian polymath Leonardo da Vinci had given his extraordinary talent and prolific output but he is only recognized for 20 paintings.

- [ ] Using a razor, Artist Vincent removed a portion of his left ear. Later on, he said he had forgotten the event.

- [ ] In Beijing's Tiananmen Square in 1989, a man stood in front of a column of Chinese Army tanks and refused to budge even though they were encircled.

- [ ] Vin Diesel went over to help with a highway car crash in 2015, and he assisted in pulling a father and two kids out of a flaming car.

- [ ] Todd Endris was lucky to have been rescued from a shark attack by a pod of dolphins.

- [ ] Above 300 trained dogs were sent to the site of the World Trade Centre collapse, to find their way through the rubble.

- [ ] Toby, a golden retriever noticed the woman's discomfort and jumped onto her chest, instantly responding as she started choking on an apple.

- [ ] Elizabeth II has two birthdays. The second Saturday in June is when people celebrate her official birthday. However, her actual birth date is April 21.

- [ ] The third President of the United States, Thomas Jefferson, introduced Mac and cheese to the American people.

- [ ] The 41st President of the United States, George H.W. Bush, did cheerleading in high school.

- [ ] Walt Disney received seven miniature Oscars in addition to one regular-sized one when he won for Snow White and the Seven Dwarfs.

- [ ] The King of Rock and Roll, Elvis Aaron Presley, did in fact have a middle name 'Aaron' rather than just 'Aron'.

- [ ] It was famous that renowned physicist Albert Einstein slept for ten hours every day.

- [ ] Robert Allen Zimmerman was the birth name of the renowned American singer-songwriter Bob Dylan.

COLOR

- [ ] There are 500 hues of gray that a normal, non-colorblind human eye can differentiate between.

- [ ] White is traditionally linked with grief and funerals rather than with joy in many Asian cultures. Therefore, Asian brides don't wear white dresses.

- [ ] Green was connected to love, fertility, and the birth of fresh life during the Middle Ages.

- [ ] White is the safest color for cars because it is more visible than the darker colors.

- [ ] Women can differentiate between more color variants than men, especially when it comes to the red-orange-yellow spectrum.

- [ ] According to research, blue is the most favorite color worldwide. People find it non-threatening and minimal negativity is attached to it in all cultures.

- [ ] Pink color is often used by therapists to deal with patients having anger issues.

- [ ] Chromophobia is a term used for the fear of color. Some colors can trigger discomfort in people having chromophobia.

- [ ] On seeing red and yellow colors together, the part of the brain that deals with hunger gets activated, and you feel hungry.

- [ ] After experimenting with light and prism, Isaac Newton created the first comprehensive color wheel in 1666.

- [ ] Due to the longest wavelength, red is the first color that a baby sees within the first few weeks of his life.

- [ ] Colors help us to remember things. Therefore, things presented in black and white tend to be forgotten more easily than the colored ones.

- [ ] Black color is associated with power. People wear black to show authority and power.

- [ ] The color of the star indicates its temperature. The hotter star appears blue, while brown or red stars are comparatively cooler.

- [ ] A chili pepper's size is a greater indicator of its spiciness level than its color. Tiny peppers are hotter than bigger ones.

- [ ] Light gives a goldfish its orange hue. Goldfish will gradually lose their color and become pale if they are kept in a dark space.

- [ ] Giraffes have a bluish-purple tongue, which is covered in long bristles that shield them from the sun.

- [ ] Flamingos' diet gives them their pink hue.

- [ ] Mosquitoes detect their victim by sensing heat. Darker colors absorb heat and thus attract mosquitoes more than lighter shades.

- [ ] The original design of the Margherita pizza was based on the colors of the Italian flag.

- [ ] Studies indicate that crocodiles are more color-blind than dogs.

COUNTRIES & CITIES

- ☐ The countries that have not adopted the metric system are Liberia, Myanmar, and the United States.

America

- ☐ 1/5th of the world's garbage is produced by Americans annually. Almost three pounds of garbage is produced by each American per day.

- ☐ Los Angeles is the short form of 'El Pueblo de Nuestra Senora la Reina de los Angeles de Porciuncula' which means 'The Town of Our Lady the Queen of the Angels of Porciuncula'.

- ☐ The US Postal Service handles almost 43 percent of the mail sent worldwide.

- ☐ An estimated 90% of taxi drivers in New York City are immigrants, with many coming from Bangladesh, Pakistan, and Mexico.

- ☐ The most consumed product in California is bottled water. The California Department of Food and Agriculture reported in 2020 that the state uses more than 2.5 billion gallons of bottled water yearly.

- ☐ The first state to install picnic tables by the side of the road, to give drivers and passengers a comfortable and secure location, was Michigan.

- ☐ Tomato juice is the official beverage of Ohio.

- ☐ Florida is the American city with the highest frequency of lightning strikes because it is situated in an area referred to as 'Lightning Alley'.

- ☐ Spitting on the sidewalk is prohibited in Norfolk, Virginia.

- ☐ Street lights were introduced in America in 1757 and the pioneer city was Philadelphia.

- ☐ It is against the law in New York State to purchase alcohol on Sundays before noon.

- ☐ The only state that shares borders with just one other state is Maine.

- ☐ According to a 2023/24 survey, dogs are the most commonly owned pets in the USA. Almost 65.1 million households own at least one dog.

- ☐ There are 13 stripes on the US flag, they stand for the original 13 states.

- ☐ Six people with the name 'Jesus Christ' have been granted driver's licenses by the state of California.

- [ ] Out of the 48 adjacent continental states, Arizona was the last to join the Union.

- [ ] Maryland does not have any natural lakes. There are rivers and various freshwater ponds in Maryland, but none of them are large enough to be considered lakes.

- [ ] Of all the states, Illinois has the most personalized license plates.

- [ ] America's farthest inland port is in Laredo, Texas. Situated on the Rio Grande, it functions as a crucial intersection for global trade and business.

- [ ] St. Louis, MO has the highest murder rate and is known as the murder capital of the United States, followed by Baltimore, MD, and New Orleans, LA.

- [ ] 'Wisdom, Justice and Moderation' - this slogan is very important since it embodies the ideals and values of Georgia state.

- [ ] Pennsylvania's highest point (Mount Davis, at 2,063 feet) is not as high as Colorado's lowest point (Arikaree River, at an elevation of around 3,317 feet above sea level).

- [ ] Moving from New York City to Los Angeles in a taxi is very expensive. It may cost you almost $8,325.

- [ ] Since 1992, hypnotism has been banned in all the public schools of San Diego.

- [ ] In America, the states that experience minimal earthquakes are North Dakota and Florida. A minor and non-damaging earthquake may occur in these states once a decade.

- [ ] The world's most fireproof capital city is La Paz in Bolivia. This city doesn't support fire because it lacks oxygen as it is located 12,000 feet above sea level.

- [ ] According to the US Census Report 2024, taking the births, deaths, and migrations into account, the US population increases by one person, every 24.2 seconds.

- [ ] The highest standardized test scores are consistently obtained by the students of Massachusetts.

- [ ] Before 1664, the New York City was known as New Amsterdam.

- [ ] It is true that the largest snowflake ever measured was 8 inches thick and 15 inches wide. In January 1887, it took place in Fort Keogh, Montana, USA.

- [ ] Indeed, California is one of the five world's leading food producers.

Andorra

- [ ] The tiny nation of Andorra, located between France and Spain, has the longest average life expectancy at 83.49 years.

Antarctica

- [ ] Antarctica's international phone dialing code is 672. Since Antarctica is a continent rather than a country, it does not have a country code.

- [ ] The only continent where no Lepidoptera (winged insects) have been discovered is Antarctica. Because of the severe weather and dearth of vegetation, Antarctica is a difficult place for insects to live.

- [ ] The only continent without land areas below sea level is Antarctica.

- [ ] There are no reptiles and snakes in Antarctica because these species need external heat to regulate their body temperature.

- [ ] With average winter temperatures of -50°C (-58°F) and summer temperatures of -12°C (10°F), Antarctica is truly the coldest spot on Earth.

- [ ] It is true that a thick layer of ice covers much of Antarctica—roughly 98% of the continent.

Africa

- [ ] More area is classified as wilderness in North America than in Africa. In Africa, it's 28% while it is 38% in North America.

Australia

- [ ] Australian notes are wear- and tear-resistant because the $5 to $100 Australian notes are made up of plastic.

- [ ] There are no trees in the 100,000 square miles area of Nullarbor Plain in Australia.

- [ ] Tasmania, Australia has the purest air in the world. Thanks to its geographic location, strict environmental laws, and minimal industrial activity.

- [ ] In the entire Australian continent, no volcanic activity has even been recorded.

- [ ] During the summer, Australia as a continent requires both a vertical and horizontal time zone.

Canada

☐ No nation has more donut shops per capita than Canada has.

☐ In Canada, moose are involved in 0.3% of all traffic accidents. This corresponds to around 430–500 collisions involving moose every year.

Chile

☐ It has never rained in the city of Calama, Chile. It is one of the driest cities in the world located in the Atacama Desert.

China

☐ More people speak English in China than in the US. China has around 900 million English learners, which is in fact more than the projected 280 million English speakers in the United States.

☐ China has an annual tobacco use per person of 1,800 cigarettes. As a matter of fact, about 350 million people, or almost 28% of the population, smoke in China.

☐ The primary cause of death in China is respiratory disease. Every year, chronic respiratory diseases (CRDs) cause around 1.4 million deaths nationwide.

☐ Skiing was not a popular sport in China. However, its popularity is increasing every year. In the year 2022/23 there were 20 million skiers in China.

☐ The price of BMW top-of-the-line 760Li is $200,000 which is more than the lifetime earnings of almost all the people in China.

☐ The 2010 Beijing traffic bottleneck continued for nine days. Other estimates place the length of the congestion at about 65 miles (105 km).

Denmark

☐ It appears that Denmark does not view jail escape as a criminal offense.

England

☐ Annually hosted in Brockworth, England, the Cooper's Hill Cheese-Rolling and Wake is a delightful event in which people chase cheese rolled down a steep hill.

☐ About 15,000 of these restaurants are in London which is more than the number of Indian restaurants in Delhi and Mumbai.

Ethiopia

☐ One of the world's oldest calendars still in use is the Ethiopian calendar that is 7 to 8 years behind this one.

☐ The Danakil Depression, in Ethiopia, is the hottest place on Earth.

Falkland Isles

☐ The population in the Falkland Isles is 2,000 whereas it has more than 700,000 sheep. It means the ratio between the human and sheep populations is 1:350.

Finland

☐ Finland boasts about 178, 947 islands, according to data.

Germany

☐ Germany is a country with an extensive number of theaters, museums, and libraries. The German government has great support for Art and cultural activities.

☐ Germany's borders are shared by nine different nations.

Greece

☐ The record of the longest national anthem with 158 verses is held by Greece. Whereas Japan has the fewest lines—just four.

☐ In ancient Greece, the term 'idiot' meant 'a private citizen'.

Hawaii

☐ Hawaii is the only US state that produces coffee. Hawaiian coffee is popular for having a unique scent and flavor.

☐ In actuality, Hawaii is moving northwest at a pace of around 5-7.6 cm (2 to 3 inches) per year, or the distance between Honolulu and Tokyo.

☐ A British explorer James Cook named the Hawaiian archipelago as the 'Sandwich Islands' after the name of one of his patrons Earl of Sandwich.

Hong Kong

☐ Hong Kong is the city with the most Rolls-Royce cars per person.

Iran

☐ The percentage of female graduates of science, technology, and mathematics, in Iran, is 70.

India

☐ Founded in 1968, Auroville is a distinctive township in India without any money or religion.

☐ Among all the nations, the minimal amount of meat per capita is consumed by India.

☐ India is known for its love of spices and produces more than 95% of the world's chilies.

☐ Some playing cards are round in India, Unlike the common rectangular cards used worldwide.

Italy

☐ About 120 little islands make up the city of Venice, which are connected by 400 bridges.

☐ Mario Rossi is the most occurring name in Italy.

Jamaica

☐ World's largest number of churches per square mile are present in Jamaica.

Japan

☐ Japan's history spans 15 million years, making it the oldest country since 660 B.C.

☐ With only about 100 inhabitants, Cat Island in Japan is a unique travel destination with a very low human population. But for every person, there are at least ten cats. This means that the island is home to a whopping 1,000 or more cats.

Korea

☐ In North Korea it is considered rude to write someone's name with red ink.

Lithuania

☐ With a death rate of 28.4 per 100,000 persons in 2020, Lithuania has the world's highest suicide rate, according to the World Health Organization (WHO).

Libya

☐ Libya is frequently regarded as one of the hottest places on earth, especially during the summer.

Nepal

☐ Nepal's flag is the only flag in the world that is not rectangular. It consists of two asymmetrical triangles.

Netherlands

☐ There is only one nation that has a national dog: the Netherlands. The national dog breed of the Netherlands is the Dutch Shepherd.

New Zealand

☐ There are only about four million people and 70 million sheep in New Zealand, it is obvious that sheep dominate the environment.

Pennsylvania

☐ A distinctive natural landmark in Pennsylvania, Ringing Boulders Park is home to stones that, when hit with a hammer, emit a sound like a bell.

Peru

☐ The mysterious 'Rainbow Mountain' in Peru is attracting scientific interest because of its remarkable striped look.

Rome

☐ Except for Antarctica, every continent has a city or town named Rome.

Russia

☐ Russia's country code is '007'.

☐ When the Bolshevik Revolution occurred in 1919, Russia was split into eleven time zones.

Saudi Arabia

☐ The largest nation in the Middle East, Saudi Arabia, lacks any perennial rivers.

Spain

☐ Spain is the second largest country to produce and export corks globally.

Sweden

☐ Sweden had the lowest murder rate per capita of any European nation in 2020, with 47 recorded murders which is amazingly low.

Switzerland

☐ Flags are usually rectangular but the only nation with a square flag is Switzerland.

Sudan

☐ Sudan indeed has more pyramids than Egypt. The ratio is about 1:2.

Tasmania

☐ Tasmania is known for having some of the world's purest and cleanest air.

Turkey

☐ In the 16th and 17th centuries, during the reign of the Ottoman Empire, drinking coffee was banned and the drinker was sentenced to death.

☐ Turkey has a river, city, district, and province named Batman.

☐ In Turkey, throwing away bread is considered to bring misfortune. It is the reason old bread is hung on to fence for birds and not thrown in bins.

☐ The dynamic city of Istanbul, which stands atop two continents, is a singular phenomenon in the globe.

☐ Reports state that the Turkey nation leads the world in tea consumption per person. A Turkish person drinks about seven pounds of tea annually on average.

Vatican City

☐ Vatican City, with about 0.17 square miles (0.44 square kilometers), is the tiniest nation on earth.

FOOD & DRINK

- [ ] During his entire life, an average person will eat 2200 chickens, 9 whole cows, and 63 turkeys. It is a rough estimate and may vary slightly depending on a person's dietary habits and natural habitat.

- [ ] An ordinary person will eat around 117 pounds of insects in his lifetime. This consumption may result from consuming processed foods or fruits and vegetables containing tiny pests and insects.

- [ ] An ordinary human being is supposed to take 13,800 chicken eggs in his life. It may seem astonishing to listen at first, but a person consumes around 250 to 280 eggs per year, adding up to thousands in his life.

- [ ] Over the course of a lifetime, an individual consumes around 113 gallons of ice cream. Ice Cream is among the most consumed desserts all over the world. The amount may exceed for someone who is excessively fond of it.

- [ ] On average, a person eats 4.4 tons of frozen food throughout his life. Thanks to the technology, it includes not only the packed frozen items but also the frozen daily meals for future use.

- [ ] Generally, a person consumes 13.5 tons of vegetables in his lifetime. The estimate is based on the percent daily consumption of vegetables, which may vary from person to person.

- [ ] The fact is that 27% of food in wealthy nations is wasted.

- One drinks around 13,000 gallons of water and 1500 gallons of milk in his entire life. Eight glasses of water daily provide the necessary hydration, while milk consumption indicates its significance in one's diet.

- The human body consumes about 75 tons of food during the entire life. It means the human body processes around 150,000 pounds of food, generating around 60 million calories in your lifetime.

- The average use of oil in your life amounts to approximately 61,000 gallons. The consumption includes not only the edible use of oil but also its usage in fuel for transportation and machines.

- A person eats around 15,000 sandwiches in his lifetime, except for the one who dislikes them. It may be due to the fact that sandwiches are easy to make and handy for those who are busy.

- Based on an estimate, a person may eat 1.7 tons of cookies in his lifetime. There will be hardly any person who dislikes cookies with the variety of options and flavors they offer.

- Carnauba wax is, in fact, the reason for the unique sheen of many fruit-flavored sweets. This wax is also used in cars.

- Only 5 animal species and 5-10 plant species provide us with over 75% of the food we eat.

Apple

- About 25% of an apple's volume is made up of air, which makes it float on water by nature.

- Eating a fresh apple may be more beneficial than consuming coffee due to the sugar present in it.

- It would take around twenty and a half years to sample every apple type if you tried a new one every day.

Almond

- Almonds are not true nuts, rather they belong to the family of peaches, cherries, apricots, roses, and plums.

Avocado

- Birds may be harmed by the poisonous substance Persin found in avocados.

Banana

- In fact, one of the most widely consumed fruits in the US is the banana.

Burger

☐ A single fast-food burger may originate from 100 different cows.

☐ With a staggering $1,768 price tag, the Galmburger is undoubtedly the priciest burger in the world.

Cake

☐ The original pound cake recipe called for a pound of sugar, butter, and eggs.

Carrot

☐ When a diet rich in the beta-carotene that is found in carrots is consumed. It may cause the skin to turn orange.

☐ A medium-sized carrot has only 25 calories and no fat.

☐ The Greeks valued the potential health advantages of carrots and cultivated them first as a therapeutic herb.

Cauliflower

☐ Beyond its well-known white appearance, cauliflower is a diverse vegetable that appears in a range of colors.

Chewing Gum

☐ The history of chewing gums can be traced back to some 9,000 years. At that time, this gummy substance was derived from a tree's resin.

☐ Eating chewing gum while cutting an onion will prevent you from shedding tears.

☐ Modern chewing gums are made up of polyisobutylene - a synthetic rubbery material.

Cheese

☐ There are approximately 1,800 different kinds of cheese worldwide out of which 1,200 types are boasted by France alone.

☐ More cheese is consumed by French people than by any other nation on the globe. Almost 57.9 pounds of cheese is consumed by every person, every year, in France.

☐ Cheese is one of the foods that people steal the most around the world.

☐ In the late 1800s, Switzerland invented the first processed cheese commonly known as 'American cheese'.

- In Serbia, it's prepared from the milk of Balkan donkeys and known. as a national treasure. Pound for pound, it costs almost $1,000.

- One plant-based ingredient included in some shredded cheese products is cellulose, which is made from wood pulp.

Chicken

- Chicken is loved by humans in every form. We consume it before its birth (egg) and after its death (meat).

Chili

- The primary ingredient in chili peppers, capsaicin, acts by attaching itself to pain receptors in the throat and mouth.

Chocolate

- During the production process, by mistake, tiny insects get into the chocolate bars. So, almost each chocolate bar has 8 legs of insects in it.

- Chocolate is poisonous for dogs. It adversely affects their hearts and nervous systems and becomes the reason for their death.

- An average American eats 10,000 chocolate bars in his lifetime equivalent to 11 pounds per capita per annum.

- It's common to mistake white chocolate for another kind of chocolate, but in reality, white chocolate lacks cocoa solid. Still, it tastes amazing.

- In reality, recycled Kit Kat bars are used to make the wafer crisps inside of Kit Kat bars.

- In pre-Columbian South American and Mexican civilizations, chocolate utilized as currency and even as a means of paying taxes.

Coca-Cola

- From 1885 to 1903, Coca-Cola contained Coca, which is made up of cocaine. However, now coca leaf extracts are added to the formula but without cocaine.

- Coca-Cola's original color before adding artificial coloring is greenish-yellow.

- As per the World Population Review 2024, US citizens consume the most Coca-Cola per person followed by the Mexicans.

- In 1940s, a special production of colorless Coca-Cola was done at the request of the Soviet Union's Marshal.

□ When Coca-Cola was advertised for the first time in 1886, it was advertised as a 'brain tonic and intellectual beverage'.

Coffee

□ A Japanese chemist Satori Kato, in 1901, developed the first soluble coffee powder.

□ It's thought that chewing coffee beans is a traditional treatment for foul breath.

Cracker

□ It is true that the holes in the crackers are essential to their baking process. These holes help keep crackers from getting blown up.

□ In actuality, crackers may have a more substantial effect on oral health than sugar.

Egg

□ One way to test an egg's freshness is to put it in a glass of cold water and see if it floats.

□ Ostrich eggs are large. Thus, they take longer to cook than other eggs.

□ Hard-boiled eggs spin more easily because their white and yolk are usually harder and drier. Soft-boiled are less likely to spin smoothly.

Eggplants

□ New Jersey is a great site to grow eggplants. It produces two-thirds of the world's eggplant.

French Fries

□ Instead of ketchup, some individuals dip their french fries in mayonnaise.

□ The origins of French fries can actually be traced back to Belgium in the 17th century.

□ Crisps, another name for potato chips, are unquestionably a popular snack all around the world.

Garlic

□ From the total garlic production worldwide, China grows almost 80%, which makes China the world's top garlic producer.

□ The body absorbs the qualities of fresh garlic when it is applied to certain sites such as feet.

Grape

☐ If you microwave grapes, they can spark or even explode. It can be dangerous and burn your microwave - so do not try it at home.

Hazelnut

☐ Nutella, the popular chocolate hazelnut spread, uses almost 25% of all hazelnuts produced worldwide.

Honey

☐ Honey doesn't spoil ever. Bacteria and yeast don't like it there. It's the only food that you can store for unlimited time.

☐ Honey typically takes 20 minutes to enter your system after eating.

Ice Cream

☐ With popularity among 81% of people, vanilla has become the most-liked ice cream flavor in the world.

☐ The avocado, garlic, chili, licuorice, Stilton cheese, and bacon are the strangest and most unique combination of flavors of ice cream.

☐ In 1904, the globe saw the introduction of the first ice cream cone.

Jam and Jelly

☐ Jam is created using sugar, crushed or puréed fruit, and sometimes pectin; jelly is usually made with fruit juice and sometimes pectin.

Kale

☐ Pizza Hut bought the most kale in the country prior to the kale craze of 2010, but they just used it as a garnish on their salad bars.

Lemon

☐ A strawberry only has 40% sugar, whereas a lemon has 70% sugar.

Milk

☐ Allergies to cow's milk are among the most common food allergies worldwide. Up to 7% of newborns are allergic to it.

☐ Camel milk's constitution prevents it from coagulating and curdling spontaneously.

☐ Despite being a byproduct of the butter-making process, buttermilk does not contain butter.

Meat

☐ Goat meat is a popular food and is the most commonly consumed red meat. Almost 63% of the red meat eaten globally is goat meat.

Non-Dairy Creamer

☐ Non-dairy powdered creamers can catch flame however, liquid creamers are safe to use.

Nutmeg

☐ If injected directly into the vein, nutmeg is exceedingly poisonous. It contains myristicin, which can be poisonous.

☐ The popular spice nutmeg, which is frequently used in baked products and pastries, has an unusual substance called myristicin.

Pea

☐ Peas were discovered 10,000 years ago, regarded as one of the earliest vegetables to be produced.

Peanut

☐ One of the components of dynamite is peanuts. The explosive component of dynamite, nitroglycerin, is made from peanut oil.

☐ Pistacia vera, a fruit tree, is the true parent of pistachios. In the same way, peanuts are legumes, a kind of fruit related to the pea family.

Pepsi

☐ Pepsin was once a component of Pepsi; hence Caleb Bradham named his invention 'Pepsi-Cola' in 1898 in reference to the word 'pepsin'.

Pineapple

☐ To minimize the sourness of a pineapple, add a little salt to it and taste the magic, it will become sweeter.

☐ More than a third of the world's pineapple supply comes from Hawaii, a major pineapple producer.

☐ In fact, according to botany, pineapples are not categorized as fruits but rather as a combination of small berries known as 'fruitlets'.

Pizza

☐ Banana Pizza is Sweden's signature pizza with banana topping on it.

- [ ] The world's priciest pizza is made in a private residence by three chefs in 72 hours. This pizza that costs an astonishing $12,000.

- [ ] The Queen Margherita of Savoy is the inspiration behind the naming of the Margherita pizza.

Potato

- [ ] French fries are so popular in the US that 1/3rd of the potatoes grown in the country are sold as frozen French fries.

- [ ] An average person in Belarus consumes 155kg potatoes per year. This is the highest consumption rate worldwide.

- [ ] With Wisconsin's assistance, the potato became the first vegetable to be grown in space.

Ranch Dressing

- [ ] In fact, ranch dressing is made using common pigment titanium dioxide. Moreover, food coloring, cosmetics, and even paper goods contain it.

Soft Drink

- [ ] Yes, orange juice is listed as an ingredient on the label of the well-known soft drink with a citrus flavor, Mountain Dew.

- [ ] Tonic water, a carbonated beverage, can glow in dark.

Strawberry

- [ ] It is true that strawberries have seeds on the outside, which is unique from other fruits.

Tomato

- [ ] Finding out that until the 1800s, Europeans thought tomatoes were harmful is fascinating.

Watermelon

- [ ] Watermelons are sometimes cultivated in rectangular shapes in Japan; these are referred to as 'square watermelons'.

☐ Have you ever tried to keep your eyes open while sneezing? It is almost impossible!

☐ You cannot tickle yourself because our brain blocks out the tickling input making it difficult to feel the tickle.

☐ An enormous amount of time is spent by people seeking lost objects; this lost time can significantly disrupt daily routines.

☐ Adults yawn roughly twenty times a day, according to research, some yawn more frequently than others.

☐ Over her lifetime, the average woman can spend up to 76 days searching through her handbag in an attempt to find a certain item.

☐ Even in today's sensible world, around 14% of the facts are fabricated, and the best part is that 27% of people are fully aware of them. Although the percentages may vary, it indicates how people can be misguided as they never think logically.

☐ Ketchup was first marketed as a medicine in 1830 in Europe and the US. It was believed to have many health benefits and a cure for skin and stomach disorders.

- [ ] An average person laughs ten times daily, as it is one of the best remedies for overcoming anxiety. A person may laugh more or; less from the estimate, depending on the person's age, occupation, and situation.

- [ ] In an unusual incident in a hospital in Las Vegas in 1980, several workers were suspended after being found guilty of putting bets on critical patients as to when they would die.

- [ ] It is astonishing to know that sugar was made a part of chewing gums by a dentist, William Semple, in 1869. Although the gum was not as sweet as now, its other ingredients were charcoal and chalk. It was made for the purpose of cleaning teeth.

- [ ] According to a survey, around 40% of guests in your house party try to peek into your medicine drawer and cabinets. It's a considerable proportion of people who are curious to know about your secrets or problems.

- [ ] The number of people opting for blue toothbrushes surpasses those going for red color toothbrushes. The reason for this is the psychology of people considering blue color as an indication of cleanliness and soothingness.

- [ ] Many people thought that John Dillinger, the bank robber, was a professional baseball player. Few people are aware, though, that before his criminal career, he had a strong love for baseball.

- [ ] According to estimates, the average person works 90,000 hours a year, or roughly ten years of his life. In addition, he dedicates a year of his life to traveling to and from work.

- [ ] About 71% of the office workers readily agreed to reveal their computer passwords for only a chocolate bar, a finding based on a survey. The survey was conducted in 2004 in London.

- [ ] The most significant number of collect calls were reported on Father's Day out of all occasions. Although collect calls are now outdated, these findings were revealed by communication companies.

- [ ] In the United States, it's costlier for you to buy a new car than it would have cost Cristopher Columbus to carry out his three voyages to and from the newly discovered world, and that also fully equipped.

- [ ] The study of the bible tells us that the chicken came before the egg. According to Genesis 1:20-22, God first created the creatures of sea and land and then ordered them to multiply.

- [ ] The cost of production of one penny is more than its face value. It takes about 3.07 cents to make a single penny.

- [ ] For a very long time, sailors thought that wearing a gold earring would improve their vision.

- [ ] Cars were considered a more environmentally friendly substitute for horses at the beginning of the 20th century. The reason was the massive dirt and excrement from horses.

- [ ] Google's Mountain View, California headquarters started using goats for land management to keep their lawns in good condition in 2007.

- [ ] Before becoming a well-known candy, M&Ms were first produced for the US Army in World War II.

- [ ] One of the places where individuals can pronounce names without moving their mouths is Hong Kong.

- [ ] The production budget of the film was almost $200 million. On the other hand, Titanic was built for about $7.5 million (about $150 million in today's money).

- [ ] A McDonald's salad may include 38 grams of fat, more than 840 calories. On the other hand, almost 540 calories, and 33 grams of fat is present in a burger.

- [ ] Fear actually helps your vision. This is due to a temporary suppression of the brain's default mode network,

- [ ] The Zombie Apocalypse Plan was created by the Washington State Department of Health as a humorous survival aid.

- [ ] There are six people who are genetic copies of you because they resemble you. People refer to them as your 'Doppelganger'.

- [ ] The fact that 72% of people will eavesdrop on someone illustrates how common this occurrence is.

- [ ] The United States made an effort to teach bats to drop 'bombs', or small explosives, on enemy locations during World War II.

- [ ] The 'anti-comet' treatment was thought to provide protection from comet impacts and dates back to ancient China and Europe.

- [ ] In the Arctic due to its extremely low temperature, it's customary to use refrigerators to pause the freezing process.

- [ ] Columbus originally thought the Earth was pear-shaped.

- [ ] Costs for nutrient-dense meals might range from 2-10 times higher than those for junk food.

- Initially, Gas masks and umbrellas were advertised as comet protection.

- Although they are frequently linked to women's apparel, high heels were really created with males in mind who rode houses.

- It is believed that a cow can be led upstairs easily but cannot be forced to lead downstairs. In fact, a cow may find it challenging to go downstairs due to its body structure, but when forced, it can indeed walk downstairs.

- In 1867, the US paid Russia $7.2 million against the 600,000 square miles of Alaska, amounting to only 2 cents per acre. The deal was made mutually after an agreement between the two nations.

- Due to a coin shortage in 1861–1862, America issued a 5-cent note. The bill was introduced to make up for the shortage caused by people storing coins during the Civil War.

- Trying to justify our laughter might intensify the bodily reaction and make it more difficult to stop.

- [ ] Mexico is, slowly and continuously, sinking at a rate of 10 inches per annum. The city is located on a former lake bed, and the increased demand for water has led to the over-extraction of water underneath.

- [ ] Earth contains 71% of water in oceans, rivers, and other water sources, while the glaciers and polar regions account for 1.7% of water in the form of ice.

- [ ] The driest state in the US is Nevada, with an average annual rainfall of about 7.5 inches (19 cm). The greater part of Nevada comprises deserted areas.

- [ ] The highest waterfall in the world, the Angel Falls of Venezuela, is 20 times higher than the famous Niagara Falls. It has a height of about 3,212 feet.

- [ ] Amazon is the world's largest river, with a length between 3,899 miles (6,275 km) and 4,345 miles (6,992 km). However, there is a debate among experts about whether the Nile River is longer than the Amazon River.

- [ ] Mongolia is the largest landlocked country in the world. It doesn't have any direct coastline and is surrounded by land from every side.

- [ ] The total number of islands in the Philippines is 7641, out of which only about 460 islands are larger than 1 square mile in area.

- [ ] Vatican City is the smallest country in the world in terms of population and area. Its population is confined to merely 800-100 people, and it only covers an area of 108.7 acres.

- [ ] With regard to the total area, England is smaller than the state of Florida. Florida's total area is 170,000 square kilometers, while England's total area is 130,000 square kilometers.

- [ ] The mass of the Earth is about 5.97×10^{24} kilograms, or you can say about 6,588,000,000,000,000,000,000,000 tons.

- [ ] The total length of the River Nile is long enough not only to cover the journey from New York to Los Angeles but also to surpass it by more than 1200 miles. River Nile is approximately 4,135 miles long.

- [ ] It is estimated that only 5% of the oceans on Earth have been fully explored by humans and the remaining 95% are unexplored.

- [ ] The detailed imaging of only 26.1% of the seafloor has been mapped as of June 2024.

- ☐ Compared to regular seawater, Dead Sea is over ten times saltier.

- ☐ The only country to enjoy the sunrise and sunset in two different oceans is Panama. Here the sun rises from the Pacific Ocean and sets in the Atlantic Ocean.

- ☐ If Earth were completely flat and free of any mountains, hills, or valleys. The Earth's surface would consequently be nearly entirely covered in water.

- ☐ The word 'Pacific', of the Pacific Ocean, is derived from the Latin word 'pacificus', which means 'peaceful'.

- ☐ Natural Resources Canada estimates that the nation is home to 20% of the world's freshwater resources that are renewable.

- ☐ Scientists believe that 20 volcanoes are erupting on land somewhere in the world on any given day.

- ☐ Over half of all volcanoes on Earth are surrounding the Pacific Ocean, a phenomenon known as the Pacific Ring of Fire.

- ☐ The August 27, 1883, explosion of the Krakatoa volcano produced the loudest sound in recorded history.

- ☐ As per the United States Geological Survey (USGS), the daily estimated number of earthquakes is roughly 50,000.

- ☐ Because of its unequal mass distribution and the associated variations in gravitational forces, Earth is not a perfect sphere.

- ☐ Estimates place daily evaporation at 8.5 million tons, a startlingly large amount when compared to other lakes.

- ☐ The ocean's average depth is an astounding 2.7 miles (4,380 meters).

- ☐ The Dead Sea, which lies in the Arabian Desert between Israel and Jordan, is a saltwater lake rather than part of the sea.

- ☐ Indeed, the Dead Sea is renowned for its extraordinary buoyancy, which makes it the perfect place for rest and flotation therapy.

- ☐ A specific water mass takes 1,000 years to complete its circle around the globe on the ocean conveyor belt.

- ☐ Mount Davis (the highest point in Pennsylvania) is situated at a height of approximately 3,213 feet, which is lower than the lowest place in Colorado, which is 3,317 feet.

☐ Saltwater oceans, which make up roughly 71% of the planet's surface, provide over 97% of the water used worldwide.

☐ Just around 5 percent of the ocean floor has been fully mapped; the remaining 95% of the seafloor is still unknown and unstudied.

☐ With a maximum depth of almost 36,000 feet, or 10,973 meters, the Mariana Trench is, in fact, the lowest place in the ocean.

☐ Asia occupies almost 30% of the planet's surface area and 60% of the world's population.

☐ North Americas' geographical center is the town of Rugby, North Dakota. In January 1931, it was determined and since then a monument on this spot has become a tourist attraction.

☐ The geographical center of the U.S. is Butte County, South Dakota, as claimed by geologists after a geological survey in 1959. A stone monument is installed to mark the exact center in the town of Belle Fourche.

☐ Denmark's Greenland is the world's largest island with an area of about 2.166 million sq/km.

☐ You can never be at a distance of more than 85 miles from a great lake in Michigan, no matter where you are in the state.

HACKS

- ☐ Freeze the gum with an ice cube. It will get harder, making removal easier.

- ☐ Clear nail polish can be used as an easy fix to quickly waterproof small goods from water or light moisture exposure.

- ☐ The combination of cornstarch and water behaves like a liquid in mild flow conditions and like a solid in rapid-force situations, like when it splashes.

- ☐ Did you know that the green, leafy top of a strawberry may be removed using a straw?

- ☐ You can keep rubber bands in the refrigerator to extend their shelf life.

- ☐ A little-known trick is to polish cutlery and leather shoes by using the interior of a banana peel.

- ☐ Certain toothpastes are also useful for lightly scratching soft plastic or metal surfaces.

- ☐ To keep the fruits and vegetables fresh in your refrigerator, place a paper towel under them. The towel will soak up excessive water and prevent them from rotting.

- ☐ You can remove minor scratches on the wooden furniture by rubbing a walnut.

- ☐ Squeeze a lemon on the avocado to keep it fresher for longer and enhance its taste. The citric acid in lemon or lime juice prevents the fruit from going brown.

- ☐ Vinegar is an amazing ingredient to remove limescale buildup on showerheads, tiles, and faucets.

- ☐ Covering the banana stem with aluminum foil slows down the ripening process, hence increasing their shelf life.

- ☐ A small quantity of mayonnaise can remove the water marks left on the wood by cups and glasses.

- ☐ Rubbing alcohol is an excellent remedy to remove paint stains from clothes.

- ☐ Crayons are a backup for candles. You can light them on top and enjoy a 30-minute light.

- ☐ The burning sensation after cutting hot peppers can be minimized by rubbing vegetable/cooking oil on your hands.

- [ ] Chopped potatoes can absorb excessive salt from soups and stews.

- [ ] Eating a spoonful of peanut butter can stop hiccups.

- [ ] Chopping a chilled onion or using a damp knife for chopping helps in reducing the tears.

- [ ] A slice of bread is a good tool to pick up small pieces of glass. Whether it be white, brown, or multigrain bread, it holds the glass pieces effectively.

- [ ] If your dog is barking at the vacuum cleaner because he is afraid of it, yell at the vacuum, and your dog will become calm and relaxed.

HISTORY

☐ About 24,000 different kinds of butterflies can be seen portrayed and explored in Egyptian art and frescoes at Thebes. These masterpieces date back to around 3,500 years ago.

☐ It was a common practice in the ancient Egyptian priests to pluck every hair from their bodies, including the eyebrows and lashes.

☐ The record for the shortest-ever rule is held by King Louis XIX of France, ruling the country for only 15-20 minutes.

☐ In 1666, on a windy, dry evening, the great fire of London broke out, leaving 85% of the population homeless. But, luckily, only six people were recorded dead.

☐ The ancient Egyptians mourned the death of their home cats by shaving off their eyebrows.

☐ In December 2006, Nico Surings achieved the record for the quickest barefoot run across 100 meters of ice. He took only 17.35 seconds to complete the run and set the record.

☐ A copy of the famous painting Mona Lisa was made out of toast by a Japanese artist in 1983.

☐ The unique fundraising event happened in London, where 637 people gathered dressed as gorillas to raise funds for the Dian Fossey Gorilla Fund.

☐ In 1963, Gaylord Perry said that before he hits a home run, they'll put a man on the moon. His statement shockingly got right in 1969 when, just a few hours after the first man landed on the moon, he hit his home run.

☐ In 1500 B.C., a woman with a shaved head was considered to be the ultimate standard of beauty and feminism. Women used to tweeze off their heads with golden tweezers and then use buffing clothes to give their heads a glossy, shiny appearance.

☐ Shoes were not invented for much of human history until about 7,000 BCE.

☐ The beginning of the human species would happen about forty seconds before midnight if Earth's history were compressed into a 24-hour span.

☐ The oldest object on Earth is a crystal that is thought to be 4.4 billion years old.

- [ ] The pillows in the ancient Egyptian era were made of stone or wood.

- [ ] In 400 BC, at the highest peak of prosperity, the Greek city of Sparta was home to 25,000 independent citizens and 500,000 a huge number of enslaved people.

- [ ] It is estimated that humans began eating heated food 1.9 million years ago.

- [ ] Fingerprints have been used for identification in Chinese civilization as far as 700 A.D.

- [ ] Back in the 17th century, mathematicians and experts were able to calculate the value of pi to be only 35 decimal places. However, the extracts from the data of 2021 tell us that it has now reached over 1.2411 trillion decimal places.

- [ ] In 1869, Wyoming accepted women's right to vote. By allowing women aged 21 and more to vote, Wyoming became the first state to pass such a law.

- [ ] The very first state of the U.S. to issue the first license plate on a car was Massachusetts in 1903.

- [ ] In 1994 only, out of all road accidents, the death toll of pedestrian fatalities was 397.

- [ ] It is believed that During World War II, the Oscar awards were made of wood due to the metal shortage. However, once the war was over, those awards were replaced with the real metallic ones.

- [ ] The state of Tennessee in the U.S. was known as Franklin until 1996.

- [ ] The Egyptians had a life expectancy of 30-35 years, almost 3000 years ago.

- [ ] In the late 19th century, the word 'pants' was looked upon as a dirty and vulgar word. It was by the 20th century that the word became an accepted word in everyday conversation.

- [ ] Cleopatra was not an Egyptian however she was born and brought up in Egypt. She was a member of the Greek Ptolemy family, who succeeded Alexander the Great as ruler of Egypt.

- [ ] After the atomic attack on Hiroshima, the survivors experienced many reactions and hazards. Some survivors even complained of their fingernails becoming black with slight bleeding.

- [ ] The emergence of farming aided in the transition from the Stone Age to settled city living.

- [ ] While the Egyptians were busy constructing the pyramids, the wooly mammoths were still alive somewhere on Earth. According to this fact, mammoths went extinct about 400,000 years ago.

- [ ] In the early 20th century, radium was considered to have health and beauty benefits and was used as an active ingredient in facial creams. However, by the mid-20th century, it was banned due to its hazardous effects.

- [ ] In English history, Queen Elizabeth II ruled for an amazing 70 years and 214 days. She is now the longest-reigning monarch in English history due to her longevity.

- [ ] Prehistoric homes were involved in constructing a structure out of sticks, branches, then covering it with woven leaves or animal hides like deer or goat skin.

- [ ] The first era of human history, the Stone Age (sometimes called the Palaeolithic Era), is defined by the invention of stone implements.

- [ ] It is true that Oxford University, which was established in the twelfth century, predates the Aztec civilization.

- [ ] In the Mesozoic Era, dinosaurs ruled the earth's landscapes and there would have been roughly 370 days in a year.

- [ ] Approximately 400 million years ago, enormous mushrooms dominated the planet.

- [ ] John Belville earned a living in 1836 by offering to tell people the time by serving as a human clock.

- [ ] Indeed, the Sumerians, who lived about 4500 years ago in Mesopotamia achieved great advancements in the art of keeping accurate time.

- [ ] About 6,000 years ago, the moon was first known to be used as a calendar.

- [ ] The average lifespan in the United States during the 1900s was indeed around 47 years.

- [ ] The dish, 'Bon Ami Pill', was created in 1859. They created a method that involved combining ketchup with soap to turn it into a pill.

- [ ] Massive chunks of granite and limestone were used to build the pyramids. We would not be able to do this with heavy construction equipment today.

HOLIDAY & CELEBRATIONS

- ☐ In 1836, Alabama became the first state to formally celebrate Christmas. The last one was Oklahoma in 1907.

- ☐ More emails are sent during holidays than the non-holiday period. Retailers send almost double the emails during holidays.

- ☐ According to the 2023 records, $12.2 billion was spent by Americans on Halloween.

- ☐ On Black Friday 2023, an average consumer spent almost $407.

- ☐ In the United States, on Thanksgiving Day, around 46-51 million turkeys are eaten.

- ☐ Depending on the species and growing conditions, a Christmas trees takes 4 -15 years to grow. The average time a Christmas tree takes to grow is 7 years.

- ☐ In 1950, a 221-foot-tall Christmas tree was displayed at the Northgate Shopping Center in Washington. It is the tallest tree that has ever been displayed.

- Every year, in the United States, 33 million real Christmas trees are sold.

- Twitter is a good place to discuss potential gifts for different occasions – 55% of the people do that!

- According to Adobe Analytics, in the year 2023, smartphones drove $5.3 billion of all online sales on Black Friday.

- 67% of the people have admitted that they have purchased gifts that were advertised on their social media.

- In Japan, every year 3 – 4 million Japanese families eat KFC on Christmas. The sale increases 10 times on Christmas than the rest of the year.

- Cause of eating spoiled Christmas food, almost 400,000 people get sick in the USA every year.

- Christmas is celebrated to commemorate Christ's birth. However, no one knows his exact date of birth.

- Christmas cards are the most popular seasonal cards in the US. Almost 1.6 billion Christmas cards are sold every year.

- The shopping activity increases so much during the Christmas season that almost 6,000 Visa credit cards are used every minute in the USA.

- In the early 1900s, Christmas lights were very costly and were considered a luxury item, that's why people were used to renting them rather than buying them.

- Most of the holiday decorating injuries happen in the months of November and December. 34% of these injuries are caused by falling while putting up decorations.

- In the 2024 holiday season, the busiest shopping days in the US are Black Friday, Super Saturday, and the 2 days before Christmas.

- There is only an 11% chance (1 in 10) of having 'White Christmas' in New York.

- England chooses the 'World's Biggest Liar' every year by organizing a competition. Each contestant has to tell the most convincing 5-minute-lie-story to win the title.

HUMAN BODY & HUMAN BEHAVIOR

☐ 60% of an adult male human body is made up of water. Whereas, in adult women, the value drops down to 55%.

☐ An average US citizen consumes 35 tons of food during his entire life. It's the same as digesting 6 elephants during their whole life.

☐ According to an estimation, an average American eats 35,000 cookies in his lifetime.

☐ Cold is the most common disease a person catches in his life. A person catches more than 230 colds during their lifetime. It equates to 3.5 years of suffering from a cold.

☐ During the whole life span you lose approximately 296 gallons of blood, 557 gallons of sweat, and 16 gallons of tears.

☐ According to Gyles Brandreth, an average person speaks 860 million words during his life.

☐ Usually, adults laugh only 15 times while children laugh 400 times a day. It sums up to, laughing approximately 1.3 million times or 2,800 hours during the entire life.

☐ Holding a sneeze can result in a ruptured eardrum, middle ear infection, damaged blood vessels, broken ribs, or damage to the lungs, brain, or throat.

☐ A sneeze travels at 100 mph spreading 100,000 droplets of germs, while a cough travels at 50 mph spreading 2000 - 5000 bacterial droplets.

☐ A good belly laugh increases the oxygen level and regulates the blood flow in your body. Laughing 100 times is as good as working on a bike for 15 minutes.

☐ During a 10-minute conversation, an average adult American lies three times. This behavior is followed by 60% of the population - according to research.

☐ Light does indeed come from human bodies; this is called biophoton emission. But the human body produces far less light naturally.

☐ Three to four grams of iron are found in the average human body, mostly in the form of haemoglobin in red blood cells.

☐ Your body is not normally the same size on both sides. There will be moments when your left side appears larger than your right.

- [ ] People start growing shorter rather than taller after the age of 30 or so.

- [ ] If you stretch your arms horizontally, the distance from the middle fingertip of your left hand to the right hand is almost equal to your height. Check it out!

- [ ] According to research, the ideal temperature range for falling asleep is 64 to 86 degrees Fahrenheit.

- [ ] The belly button of the average human is a habitat of 67 distinct types of bacteria.

- [ ] In every minute of the day, our skin sheds 30,000 - 40,000 dead skin cells.

- [ ] It's true that only humans have been observed to blush.

- [ ] If you close your eyes for about thirty minutes it will be equivalent to the number of blinks the ordinary human has a day.

- [ ] The average hiccup sufferer usually experiences them for five minutes.

- [ ] Humans may go for weeks without eating, but a human organism without sleep will die in ten days.

- [ ] According to research, listening to loud music might increase our thirst, which could result in people drinking more.

- [ ] It is true that losing 1% of your body's water might cause thirst.

Adam's Apple

- [ ] The Adam's apple is the common name for the thyroid cartilage. It is on the front of the neck. It has got its name from the story when Adam ate the forbidden apple and it got stuck in his throat.

Blood

- [ ] Your brain receives 750ml of blood every minute or 15-20% of the blood flow from your heart. The brain requires an amazing amount of oxygen-rich blood to meet its high metabolic needs.

- [ ] The human body loses 15 million blood cells every second. The bodies of the astronauts under study destroyed 3 million per second during six-month space missions, which is 54% higher than was usual prior to flight.

- [ ] If we measure the length of blood vessels in our body, by the time of adulthood, each of us has 60,000 miles of blood vessels.

- [ ] It is true that your heart beats for each blood drop in your body at least once every minute.

- [ ] Before it dies, each red blood cell in your body makes about 75,000 trips between the lungs and other tissues. Each of them only has a four-month lifespan.

- [ ] Water is approximately six times thinner than human blood.

- [ ] Approximately 8% of the total weight of an adult individual is made up of blood.

Bone

- [ ] 25% of a person's bones are found in their feet. This is due to the fact that the foot is a complex structure that must support the weight of the body and absorb impact when one is walking, running, or standing.

- [ ] A femur – the name of the thigh bone, which is the longest and strongest bone in the body. Due to its extreme strength, it cannot be broken or fractured easily.

- [ ] At birth, a child has approximately 300 bones. These bones gradually combine and reshape as you grow and by the time you become adult only 206 bones are left in your body.

- [ ] There are 29 bones that make up your skull. Some of them are, the cranial, hyoid, facial, and auditory bones.

Brain

- [ ] The human brain triples in size during the first year of life.

- [ ] Just 5% of your body weight is made up of your brain.

- [ ] About 75% of the human brain is made up of water, with the remaining 25% being made up of glial cells, fatty tissues, and other substances.

- [ ] 25% of a person's bones are found in their feet. Your brain consumes 25 watts of electricity while you are awake. This is sufficient energy to turn on a lightbulb.

- [ ] Information processing and transmission of messages throughout the brain and nervous system are carried out by almost 100 billion nerve cells in the human brain.

- [ ] You know, the messages the brain sends to our body - the nerve impulses travel at a speed of up to 170 miles per hour (274 km/h) between the brain and the body.

- [ ] It was discovered by the Canadian experts that Einstein's brain measured 15% broader than an average person's brain.

- ☐ Specific brain regions may become more active when we sleep than when we wake up.

- ☐ Water makes up about 70% of the structure of our brains.

- ☐ Since reading and dreaming truly employ distinct portions of the brain, you cannot read in your dreams.

- ☐ The brain is actually incapable of multitasking. In actuality, we are only quickly switching between numerous tasks.

Cheek

- ☐ The inside of your cheeks contains roughly 10% of your taste buds.

Ear

- ☐ The number of bacteria in your ears increases by 700 times in just one hour when you wear headphones. This is because the warm, humid atmosphere is perfect for the growth of bacteria resulting in ear infections, earwax buildup, and other ear-related problems.

- ☐ Ceruminous glands, which are found close to the eardrum, create earwax, sometimes referred to as cerumen. However, sweat glands contribute to the formation of ear wax.

Eye

- ☐ With more than two million functional components, the eye is the most complex part of the body.

- ☐ The size of the human eye remains the same throughout life, however, the human nose and ears keep growing.

- ☐ You only lose roughly 25% of your eyesight if one eye becomes blind, but you lose your entire sense of depth perception. Our ability to see depth and spatial awareness can be significantly impacted by losing eyesight in one eye.

- ☐ An average individual's eyes blink 6,205,000 times a year on average. It means, daily we roughly blink 17,000–20,000 times!

- ☐ The color of an average person's eye lightens as he ages. However, people with lighter color eyes can feel this change more accurately.

- ☐ Green eyes are very rare, only 2% of people possess green eyes globally. Moreover, only 9% of Americans have green eyes.

- ☐ The human eye can see light from a distance as far as 30 miles. You can try this by putting a candle in absolute darkness.

- [ ] Our eyes are able to detect three types of cone cells, leading us to see colors as red, green, and blue.

- [ ] People with heterochromia or having two distinct colored eyes, are not common; in fact, it affects only 1% people of the world.

Feet

- [ ] The human feet produce half a pint of sweat daily because they have 250,000 sweat glands, the most sweat glands than any other body part.

Finger

- [ ] Like fingerprints, everybody (even the twins) has a distinct tongue and eye-prints.

- [ ] The index finger, commonly referred to as the pointer finger, is frequently regarded as the most sensitive finger.

Hair

- [ ] A person loses almost 200 head hairs daily. Telogen effluvium is the term for this natural process wherein existing hairs are shed to make room for new ones to grow.

- [ ] A human scalp typically contains 100,000 hairs. Individual differences can cause this figure to vary greatly; some people may have as few as 80,000 hairs, while others may have as many as 120,000.

- [ ] The same material that makes up fingernails also makes up hair. Keratin is the material. Skin, hair, nails, and several other human tissues contain keratin, a kind of structural protein.

- [ ] In a year, an average person's head hair grows almost 6". According to this fact, our hair grows approximately 31 feet throughout our entire lives.

- [ ] Depending on the person and the stage of growth, a human hair strand usually lasts four to seven years on average.

Head

- [ ] A human head typically weighs 5kg or 10-11 pounds. All of this weight is supported by about 20 muscles and 7 vertebrae in your neck.

Heart

- [ ] Every day, your heart beats more than 100,000 times! It corresponds to 3,000–4,000 beats per hour. This amazing speed contributes to the 2,000 liters of blood providing your organs with the nutrition and oxygen they require to function.

- ☐ The human heart muscle contracts, pumping blood through the arteries so forcefully that it can spray up to 30 feet.

- ☐ Every minute, a human heart pumps almost 5 liters or 1.2 gallons of blood. If we put this amount of blood in an Olympic-size swimming pool for a year, it will be completely filled.

- ☐ True enough, the size of an adult's closed fist is about equal to the size of the human heart.

Knee

- ☐ Babies don't have bony kneecaps but a piece of cartilage is present in their knee joints. Kneecaps develop with time as the child is between the ages of 2-6.

Liver

- ☐ The only organ in the human body that can grow back is the liver. A person's liver will quickly return to its usual size if they donate a portion of it.

Lung

- ☐ Compared to your left lung, your right lung takes in more air.

Muscle

- ☐ It is astounding that humans can speak using a total of 72 separate muscles. Together, these muscles allow us to speak, form sentences, and use tone to express emotions.

- ☐ Smiling uses more than 40 facial muscles. Moreover, 200 separate muscles must coordinate to walk.

- ☐ There are no muscles in your fingers. Rather, the palm and forearm contain the muscles that govern and move the fingers.

- ☐ The human body has about 200 muscles that contract when someone walks.

Nerves

- ☐ At up to 400 kilometers per hour (km/h), or roughly 250 miles per hour (mph), these signals may transfer information quickly.

Nose

- ☐ Studies indicate that the human nose is capable of identifying over a trillion distinct scents.

- [ ] Smells are processed by our brains much less when we are sleeping.

- [ ] It's difficult to make a humming noise when your nostril is closed.

Nails

- [ ] Studies show that the average growth of fingernails is between 0.1 and 0.2mm, whereas toenails grow between 0.05 and 0.1mm each day – 4 times slower!

Pancreas

- [ ] Insulin is produced by the pancreas. The main job of insulin, which is released by pancreas, is to control blood glucose levels.

Rib

- [ ] An average human breathes 12 - 20 times every minute. So, your ribs move about 5 million times a year.

- [ ] Roughly, 8% of the global population is born with an extra rib.

Skin

- [ ] The surface area of an adult's skin is about 21 sq/ft and 15% of our body weight is due to the skin.

- [ ] As part of the skin's normal regeneration cycle, dead skin cells are naturally replaced by new ones. In the process of regeneration, an average person will shed 40 pounds of skin during his entire life.

Spine

- [ ] The base of the spinal cord contains the most sensitive group of nerves. In comparison to other parts of the body, the sacrum has a higher density of nerve endings.

Stomach

- [ ] The mucus is a protective layer that lines the stomach, shielding it from the extremely acidic gastric liquid that is inside it. Every two weeks, your stomach secretes a fresh coating of mucus, or else the stomach will digest itself.

- [ ] The stomach takes 3 – 4 hours to digest cow milk due to the lactose present in it.

- [ ] To digest the food and kill bacteria, your stomach secrets almost half a gallon of hydrochloric acid daily. It makes up around 14,200 gallons in your entire life.

☐ The stomach can dissolve metals. How astonishing is the presence of such corrosive acid in your stomach?

Teeth

☐ Teeth don't recover naturally like some other body parts do. They can still be fixed with dental restorations.

Throat

☐ Yes, hiccups can occur when there is an abrupt or significant shift in the throat's temperature.

Tongue

☐ In proportion to its size, the tongue is the strongest muscle in the human body. The tongue can exert a force of up to 100 grams per square centimeter.

☐ The only muscle in your body that is attached to only one point is your tongue. Because of this characteristic, the tongue possesses exceptional flexibility and mobility.

☐ Taste buds have an average lifespan of 10 days. In order to maintain a normal sense of taste, this turnover continues even in adulthood.

☐ The tongue's unique feature of being attached at only one end makes it extremely flexible and agile.

☐ Several medical sources claim that the tongue heals more quickly than other bodily parts.

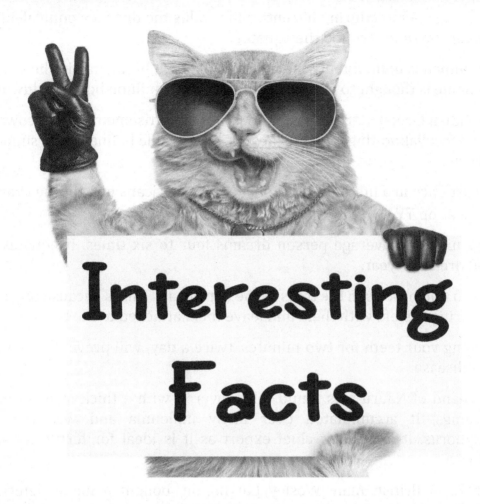

Interesting Facts

- [ ] Licking your elbow is not possible. Because our tongues and elbows are not very flexible, however, some people with extraordinary flexibility can lick their elbows.

- [ ] More zinc and copper are found in the hair of intelligent persons. Copper and zinc do, however, have significant effects on brain health and memory.

- [ ] It's shocking to find out that 13% of Americans still think that despite much scientific proof to the contrary, some parts of the moon are made of cheese.

- [ ] It's estimated that humans shed about 40,000 skin cells per hour, and these cells can quickly accumulate in our living spaces.

- [ ] You cannot fold any piece of square dry paper in half more than seven times. The physical characteristics of paper, such as its thickness and the way creases form, are to blame for this.

- [ ] Hitting your head against a wall helps to burn calories. However, this is not a recommended way to burn calories.

- [ ] An average person during his entire life walks the distance equivalent to walking five times around the equator.

- [ ] Muhammad is undoubtedly the most well-known first name in the world. This name is thought to be shared by nearly 150 million boys worldwide.

- [ ] A Canadian farmer started leasing space for advertisements on his cows in 1984. By collaborating with businesses, he was able to financially support his farm.

- [ ] At Least once in a lifetime, 1 out of every 4 Americans has got the chance to appear on TV.

- [ ] Every night, an average person dreams four to six times. It equates to 1,460 dreams a year.

- [ ] You can find oysters in the trees of the Caribbean. This is because the high tides bring oysters with them and leave them attached to the trees.

- [ ] Brushing your teeth for two minutes, twice a day, will prevent you from heart disease.

- [ ] The island of Nauru was found fully covered with a thick layer of bird droppings. It accumulated over many millennia and was rich in phosphorus. It is Nauru's chief export as it is ideal for fertilizers and explosives.

- [ ] In 2012, a British man, Wesley Carrington, bought a metal detector. Surprisingly he found gold worth £100,000 from the Roman age, within 20 minutes of his first use.

- [ ] People think their frozen bodies can be revived in the future. 500 believers, of this concept, have so far had themselves frozen in the world.

- [ ] Bill Gates predicts that there will be no poor countries left in the world by 2035.

- [ ] Cotton and linen are used to make US dollar banknotes. Because it is made up of 25% linen and 75% cotton, the paper has a distinctive texture and is quite durable.

- [ ] Refrigerating rubber bands increase their shelf life. The rubber bands will stay flexible and elastic for a longer amount of time in a refrigerator.

- [ ] Russia is home to nearly 2.6 million physicians in 2019, making up roughly 1 in 5 of all physicians worldwide.

- [ ] There is something termed 'pearl essence' in some lipsticks. This silvery material is indeed present in fish scales!

- [ ] There is a formal Bill of Rights for cows in India's Constitution. According to this bill animal slaughtering should be banned.

- [ ] Crime data show that Friday is a crime day when it comes to bank robberies, worldwide.

- [ ] One in ten individuals live on an island. Almost more than 100,000 people are living on the islands.

- [ ] It's a common belief that you may avoid crying when peeling onions while chewing a gum. The theory behind chewing gum is that it increases saliva production, which aids in the breakdown of sulfur compounds that cause tears to well up.

- [ ] Although not always in public, every US president has worn spectacles at some point in their life.

- [ ] Merely one person out of every two billion will reach the incredible milestone of being at least 116 years old. To put this in perspective, 72 years is the average lifetime for people worldwide.

- [ ] As Queen Elizabeth II's descendants, Prince Charles and Prince William have an agreement that prohibits them from traveling on the same private plane to reduce the chance of losing a future king in a single occurrence.

- [ ] Every year, an average American goes to the doctor 2-4 times. On the other hand, babies visit nine times a year.

- [ ] With around 60% of its population being male, Kuwait has the largest percentage of men. Similarly, Latvia has the highest number of females - 54%.

- [ ] An average US citizen uses 141 toilet rolls per year and almost 11,155 rolls during his entire life.

- [ ] The numbers that are divisible by 1 or the number itself are called prime numbers. The number with a 0 as its last digit cannot be a prime number.

- [ ] The world's longest-range sniper kill record is held by Ukraine. It is approximately 3,800 meters or 2.36 miles.

- [ ] By using mathematics to decode German signals during World War II, the Allies were able to breach the security of German communications.

- [ ] Zsa Zsa Gabor, a crew member of the Space Shuttle Challenger, had a cold Coke during an American Satellite bus mission in 1985.

☐ In 2021, California was declared a state with the highest number of registered vehicles. There were 31.3 million vehicles in Southern California.

☐ 'Ghost apples' occur when water freezes around an apple, causing the apple to decay inside the frozen water.

☐ There is always an even result when you add two to an even number. In a similar vein, adding 2 will turn an odd number that you start with into an odd number.

☐ In fact, the only two prime numbers that end in the digits 2 or 5 are 2. and 5. The only prime numbers that meet this requirement and have the smallest final digits being two or five are two and five.

☐ The International Telecommunication Union estimates that 49% of the world's population—3.8 billion people—did not have access to a mobile phone in 2020. They never received or made a phone call.

☐ An average American lives for almost 40 million minutes.

☐ By using human hair and ashes, diamonds can be created and set in jewelry to preserve the memories of loved ones.

INVENTIONS & INVENTORS

☐ In China, the toothbrush was invented in 1498. The United States granted a patent for the first toothbrush with bristles in the early 1800s.

☐ The first parachute was invented and tried by Louis-Sebastien Lenormand in 1783. However, its idea was conceived years ago by Leonardo da Vinci, in 1515.

☐ Percy Spencer conceived the idea of commercial microwaves when chocolate melted in his pocket while working with radar technology and microwave radiations.

☐ Lighters were created in 1823, three years before matches were manufactured in 1826.

☐ Ten-year-old Richie Stachowski has created a fascinating mask that allows swimmers to communicate underwater.

☐ China is where the paper was initially invented. And the wheelbarrow, too.

☐ One of the most extensively used calendars in the world is the Julian calendar, which Julius Caesar created in 45 BCE.

☐ Elisha Graves Otis was a key figure in the creation of the lift, which has a long history. The lift was invented by him as early as 1850.

☐ Electric chair was invented by Alfred Porter Southwick. He was a dentist, inventor, and steamboat engineer and was born in Buffalo, New York.

☐ Two of the most famous scientists married their first cousins. Charles Darwin to Emma Wedgwood in 1839 and Albert Einstein to Elsa Löwenthal in 1919.

☐ Among many other modern inventions, Leonardo Da Vinci is credited with creating the scissors and the helicopter.

☐ Sir Isaac Newton presented his laws of gravitation in 1668. However, he discovered these theories just at the same of 23, in 1666.

☐ In ancient times, people measured time with two popular devices - an hourglass and a sundial.

☐ Egypt is where the earliest sailing vessels were constructed.

☐ In 105 CE, Cai Lun, a member of the Chinese Imperial Court, created a paper.

- [ ] The first ATM was introduced in England in 1965 and was created by Scotch whisky producer and inventor John Shepherd-Barron and Ken Solutions engineer.

- [ ] The manufacturing of toilet paper can be traced back to the 14th century, when it officially started in China. However, according to historical accounts, since the 6th century cleaning with paper has been recorded.

- [ ] The first mobile phone was invented in 1973 by Martin Cooper. He made the first call with his mobile to the head of his rival project to celebrate his success.

- [ ] Due to their strict dental hygiene practices, the ancient Egyptians invented toothpaste containing rock, salt, pepper, and dried iris flowers.

- [ ] Egyptians used papyrus to produce paper, they also made rope out of papyrus fibers, which was robust and long-lasting enough to hold up their historic buildings.

- [ ] The concept of zero originated with the mathematicians and astronomers of ancient India.

- [ ] An early record player and movie projector known as the phonograph was invented by Thomas Edison.

- [ ] Louistuck's most famous creation was a unique hunting technique: after a hunt, she would cover up herself by dressing in her dog's fur.

- [ ] Lighters are older than matches in the actual invention. While matches were invented in 1826, lighters were first created in 1823.

- [ ] Braille created the raised-dot Braille system which was named after him, which enables blind people to read and write.

- [ ] ENIAC was one of the first computers. It was large—more than 8 feet high and 7 feet wide—just like a tennis court.

- [ ] In 1941, de Mestral discovered that burrs adhered to his clothes while out hunting. This realization inspired him to create the Velcro fastening technique.

- [ ] Albert Einstein was reported to need about ten hours of sleep every day in order to perform at his best.

- [ ] Tea lovers used loose-leaf tea, which took more time and effort to prepare, until 1908.

KID

- [ ] An average first-grader can identify over 200 corporate logos. This is due to the fact that logos are widely used in daily life and aim to be memorable and simple to recognize.

- [ ] Children cannot perceive size and quantity accurately till the age of 7.

- [ ] Volume of a normal person ranges between 60 and 70 decibels. A toddler from 9 months to 6 years can scream as loud as 99 – 120 decibels.

- [ ] A newborn urinates much more frequently – every 20 minutes. Whereas, a 6-month-old child urinates after every hour.

- [ ] In the first year, a baby sleeps for 11-17 hours a day. It means more than 50% of his life he spends sleeping during the first year.

- [ ] Ruth Handler created Barbie and named it after the name of her daughter Barbara. Since the doll's launch in 1959, this recognizable name has been linked to it.

- [ ] The fictional character Pinocchio was a wooden boy. In Italian, Pinocchio means 'Pine nut' or 'eyes of pine'.

- [ ] In all the Disney animated cartoon movies, one of the parents is not alive, except for 101 Dalmatians and Peter Pan.

- [ ] More than 2 billion pencils are manufactured each year in the United States. These pencils are enough to circle the world nine times if we lay them end to end.

- [ ] According to research, students, sitting in a classroom with a green view outside, perform better in their exams and remain more focused.

- [ ] Yes, during the first few weeks of life, babies actually see the world in black, white, and greyscale.

- [ ] Toddlers are known to pick up new words at a remarkable rate like they might learn as many as 10 to 15 new words every day.

- [ ] Four-year-olds ask 400 questions a day on average! It's common to refer to this occurrence as the 'Question Phase'.

- [ ] In 1965, 'Slumber Party Barbie' was released. It came with a book in its hand called 'How to lose weight'. This book included only a two-work-advice - Don't eat!

- [ ] It takes a baby at least one month to cry or release tears.

- [ ] A 13-year-old Australian boy discovered a tooth implanted in his left foot in 1977.

- [ ] Surprisingly, a standard lead pencil can write about 50,000 words (equivalent to a moderate-sized novel) or can draw a 35-mile-long line.

- [ ] The dog in the trademark symbol of an American snack food brand Cracker Jack is called Bingo.

- [ ] If Barbie was present in real life her height would be more than 7 feet and her measurements would be 39-23-33.

- [ ] Approximately 1 in every 12,000 births experiences dextrocardia, commonly referred to as right-sided heart disease.

LANGUAGE

- [ ] 'E' is the most frequently used letter in the alphabet.

- [ ] A sentence with all the English alphabet is, 'The quick brown fox jumps over the lazy dog'.

- [ ] The most spoken word in the English language is 'I'.

- [ ] The second most spoken word in the English language is 'You'.

- [ ] English has three versions – Old, Middle, and Modern English. We speak the modern English. However, if, in today's time, someone speaks old English we will not understand it.

- [ ] In English words, the letter 'w' can sometimes serve as a vowel.

- [ ] According to linguists, there may be even more spoken languages worldwide than the 41,806 recognized by the UN.

- [ ] The six official languages of the United Nations are English, French, Arabic, Chinese, Russian, and Spanish.

- [ ] On the African continent, people speak over 1000 different languages.

- [ ] Do you know what is the shortest complete sentence in the English language? It is 'Go!'.

- [ ] In the Roman alphabet, the only letter that ends on a single point is the capital letter 'P'.

- [ ] Despite their name, Arabic numerals were invented by Indian mathematicians and astronomers in the 5th century.

- [ ] Try saying: 'The sixth sick sheiks' sixth sheep's sick'. It is one of the hardest English tongue twisters!

- [ ] There are just 12 letters in the Hawaiian alphabet. The letters A, E, H, I, K, L, M, N, O, P, U, and W are the Hawaiian alphabets.

- [ ] The Chinese writing system, with more than 40,000 characters, is among the biggest and most complex languages in the world.

- [ ] In ancient times, the houses of unwanted people were burnt by the clans to force them to leave the area without shedding blood. From here the expression 'to get fired' was born.

- [ ] Russian was the first language spoken by the astronauts in space.

- [ ] Indeed, there isn't an officially recognized language in the US.

- ☐ The notion of a 'hero' is rooted in Greek literature.
- ☐ Interestingly, there is no letter 'A' in the spellings of numbers until you reach 1,000 (thousAnd).
- ☐ There are very few words that are understood worldwide, Pizza is one of them.
- ☐ The actual Egyptian language is unknown due to the decline in Egyptian temples. Today we have only assumptions.
- ☐ It is true that over 700 symbols were written in the ancient Egyptian language. We just need to keep in mind 26!
- ☐ Almost 4,000 new words are added to the English language annually. The number of terms deleted from the language in 2021 was a startling nine.
- ☐ There are about 74 million native speakers of Tamil, the oldest classical language still in use today, making it a living language.
- ☐ Grammar-wise, Korean has no direct vocabulary or grammar-wise relationship with any other language.
- ☐ A multilingual person who is proficient in speaking, reading, and writing is known as a polyglot.
- ☐ Before the Guinness Book of World Records was established, there were multiple accounts of people claiming to be polyglots.
- ☐ The record of the fastest spoken language around the globe is held by the Japanese language, with the possibility of pronouncing 7.84 syllables per second.
- ☐ Over 50% of people on the planet are multilingual. Indeed, nearly 2 billion people are thought to speak more than one language.

NATURAL PHENOMENA

- [ ] There is a cunning way to keep yourself from sinking in the quicksand: slowly raise your legs and lie on your back.

- [ ] The power released by a Category 5 hurricane is estimated to be 100 trillion watts, the same as the total nuclear arsenal of the planet.

- [ ] In a tropical rainforest, a single tree can support up to 1,000 distinct species of insects. In the tropical rainforest of the Amazon, there are almost 2.5 million species of insects.

- [ ] A lot of insects, like beetles and ants, can carry 50 times heavier objects than their body weight. It is equivalent to a person carrying two heavy cars full of people.

- [ ] About 11% of people worldwide are left-handed. This indicates that as of 2019, 717 million individuals worldwide—or roughly 6.9 billion people—identified as left-handed.

- [ ] Women blink more frequently than men, almost twice. An average woman blinks 19 times while a man blinks 11 times per minute.

- [ ] The speed of cough, coming out of your mouth, is about 60 miles per hour (96.5 km per hour).

- [ ] Studies show that an average person can usually fall asleep in seven minutes or less.

- [ ] Your heart may skip a beat and take a second to resume its regular beat when you sneeze.

- [ ] Seasons influence human growth. Springtime growth in children is usually a little faster than at other times of the year!

- [ ] If you dip pearls in vinegar, they will melt.

- [ ] Almost 8 million times a day, lightning strikes the earth and, surprisingly, 80% of the lightning victims are male.

- [ ] An adult who does hard exercises sweats up to 4 gallons per day, however, this amount decreases to 1.5 gallons when it comes to an average adult.

- [ ] Some people have an inborn tendency to ingrown toenails.

- [ ] According to the latest research, there are 10 microbes for 1 human cell in a human body. There are 10 trillion human and 100 trillion bacterial cells in the human body.

- [ ] Uncomfortable sleep triggers nightmares and a very cold room is one of the causes behind nightmares.

- [ ] Blind people, just like normal human beings, see visual scenes in their dreams.

- [ ] You cannot see red, in water, as deep as 33 feet or more. The red color turns green in the depths of water.

- [ ] Due to low pressure and low humidity, at regions higher than 12 miles, water evaporates very quickly - even from your body.

- [ ] We see colorful dreams, however, 12% of people see dreams like an old movie - completely black and white!

- [ ] Studies show that men with excessive hair on their bodies are more intelligent. However, never misjudge a person with less hair!

- [ ] Humans cannot swallow and breathe at the same time. Doing this results in choking.

- [ ] Studies indicate that dreams often endure between 2–3 seconds.

- [ ] People are unable to speak and breathe at the same time.

- [ ] It is estimated that approximately 1 in 12 males and only 1 in 200 women are color blind.

- [ ] It has been estimated that 12% of people see dreams only in grey, black, and white.

- [ ] You smell like nobody else unless you have a twin. You smell exactly like yourself.

- [ ] The lightning bolt can be approximately five times hotter than the sun.

- [ ] Yawning typically lasts six seconds; some people can yawn for up to 21 seconds or more!

- [ ] With a length of more than 14,000 miles, coral reefs are in fact the largest living structures on the earth.

- [ ] The Great Chilean Earthquake of 1960, usually referred to as the Valdivia earthquake, was the greatest earthquake ever recorded.

- [ ] June 15, 743 BC, saw the longest total eclipse in recorded history, lasting 7 minutes and 27.54 seconds.

- [ ] Astronomy estimates that it takes the Earth 23 hours, 56 minutes, and 4.2 seconds to complete one full rotation.

- [ ] Moving upward is faster for fire than moving downward.

- [ ] Because there is no gravity when astronauts are in space, their spines can grow.

NATURE & THE UNIVERSE

☐ Fire tornadoes, sometimes referred to as fire whirls can happen during very hot and intense wildfires.

☐ A lightning bolt's temperature can rise to 50,000°C, which is five times hotter than the sun's surface.

☐ The abrupt release of hot rock, gas, and ash into the atmosphere during a volcano eruption creates breathtaking lightning shows.

☐ The largest hailstone ever measured was found near Aurora, Nebraska, USA, on June 22, 2003.

☐ A mysterious occurrence known as 'ball lightning' was absorbed by scientists on a plane in 1975 while they were passing over China. It used to be a myth!

☐ 99% of the water on Earth is too salty to drink or else frozen in the form of ice and glaciers. Therefore only 1% of water is fresh and drinkable.

☐ Carbon is a major component of all living things, including humans, plants, and microbes.

- [ ] Some beaches have a glowing appearance at night caused by microscopic sea creatures, like dinoflagellates, which generate light as a defense mechanism.

- [ ] There is only 0.0003% freshwater that is both safe and readily available for human consumption.

- [ ] Between the Earth and space is a 60-mile-thick atmosphere.

- [ ] A surprising indicator that a tsunami is about to form is the unexpected retreat of ocean water on adjacent beaches; as it creates an unusual decrease in sea level.

- [ ] A moonbow is created when the moon's rays shine through the same water droplets.

- [ ] Without oxygen the sky will darken like night, hard concrete will turn to dust, oceans will evaporate, and everyone will get sunburnt on the beach in just 5 seconds.

- [ ] Coral reefs can take years for an inch of growth. Their slow growth rate leaves them especially susceptible to harm from human activity.

- [ ] The Earth is situated around 93 million kilometers away from the sun. The time takes for light to traverse this distance is roughly eight minutes and twenty seconds.

- [ ] Surface tension, which reduces the liquid's surface area, causes a liquid to spontaneously form into a spherical shape when it is floating freely in space.

- [ ] Only around 5% of the universe is regarded as 'visible matter' by modern science.

- [ ] Dark energy makes up 68% of the universe, whereas dark matter makes up 27%. Even with a telescope, these are invisible.

- [ ] If you were standing on Earth's surface, outer space would be roughly 62 miles away.

- [ ] The International Space Station completes one orbit of the planet in around 92 minutes.

- [ ] Did you know that Laika (a dog) was the first living thing in space?

Planet

- [ ] Because Jupiter has a much higher volume than Earth, it is so big that about 1,000 Earths might fit inside it.

- [ ] On Venus, a day lasts longer than an Earthly year.

- [ ] Despite Mercury, being the closest-to-the-sun planet, Venus is the hottest planet because Mercury lacks an atmosphere that helps to trap heat.

- [ ] It is now estimated that Jupiter has about 79 known moons orbiting it.

- [ ] The United States is greater than Pluto because it is so little.

- [ ] Indeed, it's sometimes claimed that scientists know more about the Moon's and Mars' surfaces than we do about the ocean floor on Earth.

- [ ] The 'rain' on Venus is composed of sulphuric acid and the 'snow' is thought to be a metallic material.

- [ ] The only planet in our solar system whose orbit is lined with its equator is Mercury.

- [ ] Venus rotates anticlockwise around the Sun. Accordingly; the Sun appears to rise in the west and set in the east on Venus.

- [ ] Two notable planets whose rotation occurs in the opposite direction of their orbits around the Sun are Venus and Uranus.

- [ ] All the planets, in our solar system, are named after an ancient mythological deity or god except for Earth.

- [ ] In 1850, planet George was renamed as planet Uranus.

- [ ] On the gas giant planet Jupiter, there is a storm known as the Great Red Spot that has been going on for the last 200 years.

- [ ] Mars's red appearance isn't just a result of rust; the planet's soil is rich in iron.

- [ ] Unlike Earth, Saturn is made up of gas, which makes it less thick that it can float on water since its density is less than water.

- [ ] Scientists have found fascinating clues that suggest life may exist on Venus in recent years.

- [ ] On Jupiter's moon Io, scientists have discovered a massive, recently active volcano.

- [ ] The greatest volcano in our solar system is, in fact, on Mars.

- [ ] One amazing truth about the Earth that defies perception is its rotation.

- [ ] In the Solar system, with reference to distance, our planet Earth is in third place, after Mercury and Venus.

- [ ] Earth revolves at a speed of roughly 1,000 miles per hour.
- [ ] On Earth, the duration of a day is indeed changing, though not always in a direct manner.
- [ ] If you weigh 100 pounds on Earth, you would only weigh 38 pounds on Mars.
- [ ] Venus's day is longer than its year due to its incredibly slow rotation period of 243 Earth days.
- [ ] The planet that is nearest to the sun is Mercury, which is the innermost planet in our solar system. However, it is unable to effectively control or insulate against temperature changes.
- [ ] Fossils of microscopic organisms have been discovered by scientists, providing proof of previous microbial life on Mars in 1986.
- [ ] The United States is larger than Pluto because of its tiny size.
- [ ] It is possible for a single season on Uranus—winter, spring, summer, or fall—to endure up to 21 years on Earth.
- [ ] Because of its red hue, Mars is sometimes linked to the Roman god of battle.
- [ ] The Martian year indeed lasts for roughly 687 days. On the other hand, Earth only takes approximately 365 days.
- [ ] Olympus Mons, the greatest volcano and canyon system in the solar system, is located on Mars.
- [ ] Red Planet Mars shows signs of a more temperate climate, complete with calm lakes, and meandering rivers.
- [ ] The gas giant planets—Jupiter, Neptune, Saturn, and Uranus—don't have solid surfaces and make it unable to walk on them.

Moon

- [ ] In 2026, NASA will send astronauts to grow plants on the moon. If all goes well, they will soon launch a lunar mini greenhouse.
- [ ] The gravitational field on the moon is only 1/6th of the Earth. A person weighing 180 pounds, weighs only 30 pounds on the moon.
- [ ] The full moon appears nine times brighter because it reflects more sunlight onto our Earth.

- [ ] For more than a billion years, the Apollo astronauts' footsteps will still be visible on the moon.

- [ ] Blue Moon is a phenomenon when there are two full moons in a single month. This occurrence happens around every 2-3 years.

- [ ] The tides in the ocean are mostly caused by the moon.

- [ ] We always see the same side of the moon, because it does not rotate on its axis.

Star

- [ ] The diameter of the sun is 864,400 miles. This is roughly 109 times Earth's diameter.

- [ ] Pistol is one of the Galaxy's brightest stars that shines with a brilliance 10 million times that of our Sun.

- [ ] It takes around eight minutes and twenty seconds for light from the sun to reach Earth.

- [ ] The diameter of the massive red star Betelgeuse is greater than the radius of the Earth's orbit around the sun.

- [ ] Only a small portion of stars can be explained by astronomers due to the vastness of space and the limitations of present technology.

- [ ] There are more stars in the sky than there are sand grains on Earth.

- [ ] The universe's average star is between 5 and 6 billion years old.

PEOPLE, CULTURE & HABIT

- [ ] Anxiety and despair are examples of negative emotions that can have adverse effects on our immune system.

- [ ] It's amazing to consider that Americans eat enough pizza every day, on average, to fill an 18-acre plot equivalent to 72 football fields.

- [ ] The number 17 is associated with misfortune in Italy. In a similar vein, the number four is unlucky in Japan.

- [ ] The well-known children's book author and artist Dr. Seuss frequently called his name '*soice*', pronounced "Zoice" by the family, and by Dr. Seuss himself.

- [ ] In America, only one in 14 women and one in 16 men are naturally blonde.

- [ ] Russians typically say, "I'm listening" when they answer the phone.

- [ ] The National Agricultural Statistics Service estimates that the US spends $203 million or more on barbed wire every year.

- [ ] In the United States, almost every person possesses two credit cards.

- [ ] Cremation is indeed a widespread funeral custom in Japan, where almost 98% of people choose this option.

- [ ] According to a survey, an average Japanese household spends more than ten hours watching television, however, the global average is two to three hours per day.

- [ ] Among the world's top yogurt drinkers per capita is Bulgaria.

- [ ] More turkeys are consumed per capita in Israel than in any other country.

- [ ] With an average of 33.3 gallons of Coca-Cola consumed annually per person, Icelanders are the world's largest Coca-Cola drinkers.

- [ ] Nearly 1 in 7 workers in Boston, Massachusetts, or 14.3% of all workers, walk to work.

- [ ] 1 in 9,000 individuals are born with albinism. This indicates that the prevalence of albinism is roughly 0.011% worldwide.

- [ ] Houston, Texas, has the highest frequency of eating out among Americans—4.6 times per week on average—with its population.

- [ ] The most common food allergy in young kids and infants is from cow's milk.

- The Czechs are, in fact, the nation with the highest per capita intake of beer among men, according to several statistics. A Czech man drinks 142.4 liters of beer annually on average.

- In the UK, the Speaker of the House of Commons is the head of the house, but parliamentary custom dictates that the Speaker cannot even vote on laws or take part in debate.

- In the US, obesity is an important public health issue. Approximately 300,000 fatalities in America are linked to obesity each year.

- Scotland is frequently referred to as the 'redhead capital of the world'. Red hair is present in approximately 13% of Scots, a percentage that is much higher than the global average of 2%.

- The English philosopher and reformer Jeremy Bentham left his will to the University of London, requiring that his skeleton be present at all of the organization's significant meetings - and now it is!

- The United Nations projects that the world's population will continue to rise, from its current 7.9 billion people to 9.7 billion by 2050 and then over 15 billion by 2080.

- In the Nebraska state of America, burping or sneezing in churches is legally prohibited.

- In Utah, swearing in front of a corpse, or desecration of a dead body is illegal.

- It is illegal to carry an unwrapped ukulele on the street in Salt Lake City, Utah.

- A long-standing rule in Quebec requires that margarine and butter must have different colors.

- In a week, an average American eats 3.66 ounces of cereals, which makes 11.9 pounds per year.

- 24,000 hours of an average American's life are spent working just to pay the heavy national taxes.

- If a Saudi husband fails to provide his wife with fresh coffee every morning, the wife has all the legal authority to get divorced.

- 80% of the American men, when asked, said that if they had to marry again, they would marry the same lady.

- 50% of American women claimed that they would choose the same partner if they had to marry again.

- [ ] According to a huge number of Americans, they loved the smell of bananas.

- [ ] According to a survey, almost 7% of Americans confessed that they never bathe.

- [ ] People in South Korea are on average 1 - 3 inches taller than their North Korean counterparts.

- [ ] There is a comedy club in Barcelona, Spain, where tablets are attached to the back of the seats. A specific laughter-detection software is installed in these tabs. People are charged 0.30 Euros per laugh.

- [ ] Almost 70% of Americans include their pet's name (as a family member) on the greeting cards.

- [ ] In a year, an average American spends 58.6 minutes waiting for a red-light signal. It equates to 6.5 months of waiting, during the entire life.

- [ ] Only 1 out of 7 burglary cases are expected to be solved in the United States.

- [ ] In a year, 680 pounds of paper is consumed by an average American. Collectively, as a nation, it sums up to 85,000,000 tons.

- [ ] In the US, more tigers are kept as pets than in the wild. The figure for pet tigers lies somewhere between 5000 - 7000.

- [ ] A company in Taiwan manufactures wheat utensils, which you can eat!

- [ ] If the 15-year or older children are caught cheating in their final exams, they can be sent to jail in Bangladesh.

- [ ] In Switzerland, making unnecessary noises between 11 pm to 6 am is illegal, including car door slams.

- [ ] In Kansas, fishing is not allowed bare-handed.

- [ ] In England, during Elizabethan times, people were used to carrying their own spoons to the invited dinners and parties.

- [ ] Prolonged sitting and no movement endanger your life. In the Western world, the number of people killed by smoking and lack of movement is the same.

- [ ] In comparison to different-hair-colored people, sensitivity to temperature and tolerance to pain is higher in redheads.

- [ ] Egyptians thought that black cats often acted as the goddess's earthly companions and even had sacred cats based in temples to fight off evil spirits.

- [ ] Sour milk has been used as a bathing remedy since ancient Egypt. It was thought that the lactic acid in milk had skin-softening qualities.

- [ ] There are 43 nations where a monarch serves as the head of state at the moment.

- [ ] The United Nations estimates that 150 million individuals worldwide are named Muhammad.

- [ ] Elderly people frequently enjoy their very salty food. The taste buds on our tongues may shrink and lose their sensitivity as we age.

- [ ] Every American use about 100 gallons of water a day on average for everyday purposes.

- [ ] Nearly half of American people, according to the data, eat at least one sandwich every day.

- [ ] In the Netherlands, the average daily consumption of coffee for each person is about 2.5 cups.

- [ ] Since 2015, it has been against the law to throw food away in Seattle, Washington.

- [ ] Each American consumes about three pounds of peanut butter annually.

- [ ] The latest estimates indicate that the worldwide sex ratio is roughly 51% male and 49% female.

- [ ] Up to 53% of women globally feel that they must apply cosmetics before leaving the house.

- [ ] Nearly half of Americans think the sun is not a star.

PLACE

- [ ] Happy Meal sales account for about forty percent of McDonald's profits.

- [ ] About 20% - 25% of the US population eats fast food daily. 7% of which goes to McDonald's.

- [ ] The minimal price of the Big Mac is in Taiwan, i.e., $2.39. Whereas, the most expensive Big Mac is sold for $8.07 in Switzerland, as of July 2024.

- [ ] There are more than 600 rooms in Buckingham Palace, the official abode of the British monarch. This magnificent home was built in 1703.

- [ ] Vermont's Montpelier is the only state capital in the union where you cannot find McDonald's.

- [ ] Richmond, British Columbia was home to Canada's first McDonald's restaurant. George Cohon owned and ran the business.

- [ ] In America, the company with the highest hiring rate is McDonald's. It hires almost 1 million people annually.

- [ ] The only moving landmark among the National Historic Monuments in the USA, are the San Francisco Cable Cars.

- [ ] The famous Starbucks in Myeongdong, South Korea has five floors.

- [ ] Despite being the President of the US, he has to pay bills for his, his family's, and guest's food and other expenses, in the White House.

- [ ] There are 13,092 cutlery utensils in the White House.

- [ ] Antarctica's Length Glacier Waterfall is a singular natural marvel. The glacier appears to be bleeding.

- [ ] Over 50 dogs tragically lost their own lives by jumping off the Overtoun Bridge in Scotland in the 1980s, the bridge has remained mysterious.

- [ ] In the Philippines, McDonald's does have spaghetti on its menu.

- [ ] McDonald's employs approximately 1.5 million people worldwide.

- [ ] The Statue is a famous representation of liberty with a seven-pointed crown.

- [ ] Because Mount Everest is located around 8.8 kilometers above sea level. That being said, this effect is minuscule, amounting to about 15 microseconds annually.

PLANTS, FLOWERS & TREES

- [ ] During the 17th century, some rare tulips were more valued than gold in Holland.

- [ ] Orchids – the largest flowering plant family with more than 25,000 species, don't need soil to grow.

- [ ] There is a plant, commonly known as 'Bird of Paradise'. Its' oddly grown vibrant flower petals resemble a flying tropical bird.

- [ ] Rose is the most-loved flower worldwide. According to the data, 85% of Americans rate roses as their first choice.

- [ ] Planting an apple seed would result in a tree that bears apples greatly different from the parent tree in terms of flavor and appearance.

- [ ] Just because people can produce alcohol from apple cider, Johnny Appleseed planted apples.

- [ ] Unlike cold water, warm water encourages faster and greater growth in plants because it allows the roots to absorb more nutrients and water.

- [ ] A bristlecone pine found in California's White Mountains is the oldest known living tree. Its approximate age is 5,000 years.

- [ ] The only vegetables that resemble flowers are broccoli and cauliflower. In particular, cauliflower is the immature flower head and broccoli is the immature flower buds.

- [ ] Snapdragon is a flower that looks like a dragon's mouth. When you squeeze its sides, it opens and closes like jaws as if it is ready to eat something.

- [ ] In ecology, the term 'duff' describes the organic waste that has decomposed on a forest floor and is frequently made up of twigs, leaves, and other plant debris.

- [ ] When leaves change color in the autumn, they finally take on their true hue. Chlorophyll causes them to turn green and conceal their true colors in the summer.

- [ ] In California, Hyperion is the tallest tree in the world with more than 360 feet in height.

- [ ] Fungus in the forests enables communication between trees and plants.

- [ ] An adult tree can create an astounding amount of oxygen—enough to support up to 20 people for a day—when it is fully matured.

- [ ] Pineapples frequently take a few years to reach maturity and start bearing fruit.

- [ ] Certain kinds of bamboo can grow up to three feet a day.

- [ ] Green places like fields are thought to have about 50,000 spiders per acre.

- [ ] Although the 700,000 leaves that mature oak trees lose each year are astounding, they are an essential element of the tree's life cycle.

- [ ] The Yew tree's fruit, bark, and leaves contain a poisonous substance called taxine that, if consumed, can be lethal.

- [ ] Unlike other living things, trees do not have a set lifespan since, in the absence of the effects of man or nature, they can grow forever.

- [ ] A plant known as a 'Pomato' is capable of yielding both potatoes and tomatoes.

RANDOM

- [ ] More cold water can be held by a sponge than hot water.

- [ ] The most often forgotten travel necessity is a toothbrush.

- [ ] The Christmas tree tradition is said to have originated in Germany.

- [ ] Using a conventional QWERTY keyboard layout, the longest word that can be typed with just the left hand is 'Stewardesses'.

- [ ] It's surprising to know that you consume approximately 1/10 of a calorie each time you lick a stamp.

- [ ] The '7' in the 7-Up logo represents the inventive spirit and diligence of its creator, Charles Leiper Grigg. Whereas the red spot in the logo represents Grigg's originality - he was an albino with red eyes.

- [ ] In the Webster's 1996 dictionary, 315 words were misspelled.

- [ ] The enormous popularity of M&Ms is shown by the fact that 200 million of the candies are sold daily in the US.

- [ ] It's shocking to learn that each year, coconuts cause more fatalities in humans than shark attacks. Statistics show that sharks kill five to six people a year, but coconuts are responsible for about 150 deaths annually.

- [ ] The World Health Organization (WHO) estimates that 14% of drug injectors have HIV infection. Drug injection provides a significant risk of HIV infection because infected needles and equipment are shared among injecting users.

- [ ] Every year, in the UK, 4 individuals pass away because of trousers. People rush to get to work in the morning and try to put on/adjust their trousers while getting down the stairs and collapsing to death.

- [ ] Jan Honza Zampa made headlines when he broke the record for the fastest beer consumption—one liter in just 4.11 seconds.

- [ ] According to scientific estimates, there could be as many as 10–30 million bug species on the globe. Therefore, the proportion of insects among all organisms may be higher than what we now think.

- [ ] Most of the insect species keep nature in balance as they consume other insects, fertilize crops, provide food for other animals, manufacture goods like honey and silk, or have therapeutic applications.

- [ ] Charles I was the shortest British king, standing 4 feet 9 inches tall.

- [ ] Trading a paper dollar for a combination of coins totaling $1 is the process of making a change for a dollar. By using pennies, nickels, dimes, quarters, 50-cent pieces, and dollar coins, we can create a $1 change in 293 ways.

- [ ] The 118 reeded edges of dimes are a defining characteristic of the Lincoln cent design. However, one distinctive aspect of the Washington Quarter is its reeded edge, which has 119 grooves.

- [ ] Abraham Lincoln was killed in 1865. Ever since, it is supposed that the White House is haunted by his ghost – the White House Ghost.

- [ ] If a healthy person tries to kill himself by holding his breath, he can only do it till he is in his senses. His body will start breathing again as soon as he is unconscious. So, technically, it's impossible!

- [ ] 56% of the words are typed by an average person's left hand on a QWERTY keyboard. At the same time, on a DVORAK keyboard, the right hand does 56% of the typing.

- [ ] The 2" x 4" size mentioned on the lumber measures 1½" x 3½".

- [ ] The US IRS agency admits that the company's error rate has increased to 30.8%. It means almost 1 out of every 3 people get wrong answers to their queries.

- [ ] Americans use so much ice in their drinks that only if they cut down 1/3rd of the amount they can be the net exporters of energy.

- [ ] Left-handed people have less life expectancy. One of the reasons is the use of equipment designed for right-handed people which kills 2,500 left-handers a year.

- [ ] An average American spends only 19 minutes reading every day. However, the period is much higher in adults over 65 years, they read about 20 books annually.

- [ ] An average American eats 3,400 mg of salt daily. However, an average Chinese consumes 17.7 grams of salt per day.

- [ ] The average lifespan of an American is 78.8 years. According to this figure, you will see almost 29,000 sunsets in your entire life.

- [ ] In our lifetime we get to interact with almost 80,000 people.

- [ ] According to a 2022 survey, an average American consumes 6 pounds of butter per day.

- [ ] An average American spends $161 on clothing, monthly. It sums up to $154,500 in a lifetime.

- [ ] According to statistics, 360,000 people are born daily, so they share the same birth date. Also, almost 151,600 people die daily.

- [ ] In your lifetime, you discard almost 63 tons of trash. However, 30% of the world's garbage is generated by Americans.

- [ ] If a person sleeps for 8 hours daily and we calculate this time for a person who lives for 75 years, it sums up to 25 years of sleeping.

- [ ] An average person spends 82 minutes on eating every day. It makes 4.5 eating years in a lifetime.

- [ ] 20% of the world's population lives on $1 a day and more than half of the population live on $10 dollars a day.

- [ ] The percentage of people infected by flesh-eating bacteria is way more than those struck by lightning. About 700 - 1100 bacterial cases are reported, whereas only 20 lightning cases are reported in the US every year.

- [ ] From 1922 to 1990, Osborne hiccupped for 68 years. It all started with an accident and became the longest hiccup span.

- [ ] The number of organisms living on our skin is more than the number of humans living on Earth. Moreover, our stomach contains 1,000 times more organisms than that.

- [ ] Chips are 200 times costlier than potatoes in the United States.

- [ ] Every year, more than a billion birds die due to collisions with windows, in the United States.

- [ ] In 2005, the firefighters used ice balls to put off the fire when they couldn't get close to the burning apartment in Sibiu Romania.

- [ ] Usually, we read the messages in the sender's voice, specifically if we know the person very well.

- [ ] Statistically, 6.1 million accidents are caused by men while 4.4 million accidents are caused by females, in the US, each year.

- [ ] An Indonesian python was discovered in 2017 with a human in its gut. The 4-year-old youngster had been completely engulfed by the 23-pound serpent.

- [ ] Numerous studies have indicated that about 2 people die every second.

- [ ] Plastic doesn't begin to degrade for 50,000 years on average.

- [ ] One billionth of a second is equivalent to one nanosecond.

- ☐ Did you know that door knobs made of copper and brass contain antibacterial qualities?

- ☐ Mabel McKay Hardiman not only survived the terrible Titanic tragedy in 1912, but she also lived through two more White Star Line ship disasters.

- ☐ The incredible event in which a flight attendant fell from a plane without a parachute at a height of nearly 30,000 feet and survived miraculously.

- ☐ From 2002 to 2004, Ian Harvey's beard, measuring 17 feet 6.6 inches (5.34 meters), was the Guinness World Record holder.

- ☐ A pack of chewing gum was the first item purchased in a supermarket in 1974 with a barcode scanner.

- ☐ A classic beer style made from fermented bananas is called banana beer.

- ☐ The proposed (IFC) International Fixed Calendar had 13 months with 28 days in each month.

- ☐ 31,557,600 is the total amount of seconds in a year that does not include leap years.

- ☐ The average rate of increase in the global population was about 215,000 each day.

- ☐ Soft drink containers made of plastic didn't start to be used extensively until 1970.

- ☐ The purpose of the expiration date on a water bottle is actually to indicate the shelf life of the container itself.

- ☐ General Foods developed the phrase, 'Breakfast is the most important meal of the day' to advertise their cereal goods.

- ☐ 5,050 is the total of all the numbers from 1 to 100.

- ☐ Tooth decay is the disease that is the most common among both kids and adults.

- ☐ The shell of an egg makes up to 12% of its total weight.

- ☐ Although the average yawn lasts roughly six seconds, it can last anywhere from three and a half seconds to significantly longer.

- ☐ China is where the largest spider fossil was found. This fossil is 165 million years old and almost one inch long.

- ☐ NASA owns its radio station called a 'Third Rock Radio'.

RELIGION & FAITH

- [ ] Benedict IX became pope when he was only 11 or 12 years old – the youngest pope ever!

- [ ] You can find two angel's names in the Bible - Gabriel and Michael.

- [ ] Almost 4,000 recognized religions exist in the world. However, the most common religions that are followed by 75% of the world's population are just 5.

- [ ] There are more than 70,000 Jedi adherents in Australia; the religion is real.

- [ ] Changing religion is a common practice in the US. According to a 2023 survey, 24% of Americans have switched their religion in their life.

- [ ] Jehovah's Witnesses believe that blood transfusion is prohibited according to the Bible. Similarly, Christian scientists often rely on spiritual healing rather than traditional medical assistance.

- [ ] The Amish community rejects the use of modern technology like electricity or telephones, as the use of technology can disrupt their way of living.

- [ ] Christianity has the largest following worldwide, followed by Islam as the second largest religion, and Hinduism ranks as the third largest.

- [ ] Buddhism started, in the 5th BCE, in India. However, nowadays, Buddhism is more popular in Cambodia than in India.

- [ ] Early Christians used a fish-like sign called 'Ichthys' instead of a cross.

- [ ] In the world, 87% - 90% of the Muslims are Sunni.

- [ ] The world's largest Sunni Muslim population, around 225 million, is in Indonesia.

- [ ] In all the Muslim countries, Shia Muslims are mostly located in Iran, Iraq, India, and Pakistan. However, the country with the maximum number of Shia Muslims is Iran with 90% – 95% Shiites.

- [ ] 'Sikh' is a Punjabi word that means 'learner' or 'follower'.

- [ ] There are almost 4 – 5 million humanists worldwide.

- [ ] Bahá'í is the youngest of all the major religions that was founded in the 19th century by Bahá'u'lláh.

- [ ] Among the entire Christian population worldwide, 33% - 40% are Protestants.

- [ ] There are 2.4 billion followers of Christianity worldwide. Within Christianity, Catholicism marks the largest domination by having almost 50% following.

- [ ] God's name is not mentioned, even once, in the Book of Esther.

- [ ] A month that starts with a Sunday, will always have a 'Friday the 13th' in it.

- [ ] Roman Catholicism is the most practiced religion in Nicaraguan, about 45% of the people are catholic.

☐ 'Jiffy' is a word used to describe a short instant – 1/100th of a second. However, it is not officially recognized but used in many fields.

☐ Although we cannot measure the weight of air in a glass of milk, it is as small as the weight of an aspirin tablet in a milk glass.

☐ Coconut water from the young coconuts can be injected intravenously, in some intense medical situations.

☐ Super glue needs moisture to stick the things together, and not the air.

☐ A small flap in the ear called tragus contains an appetite control point. It is also called the 'Hunger Point' through which you can control your hunger.

☐ 99.9999999999999% space of an atom is empty. As the human body is made up of millions of atoms, if we remove the empty parts from all the human beings in the world, nothing will be left but a sugar cube.

☐ The chemical composition of emotional tears is different than the tears caused by irritants.

☐ Wound licking is an instinctive behavior. Our saliva helps in blood clotting, aids against infections, and helps in a speedy healing process.

☐ No element name or symbol contains the alphabets 'J' and 'Q' and thus these two alphabets are absent from the periodic table.

☐ Sound travels through water at a speed of around 4.3 times that of air.

☐ Sound waves can heat the air they travel through; this is known as sound heating.

☐ The air pressure differential between two straws in your mouth causes a sort of 'competition' for the liquid when they are placed side by side.

☐ A regular soda can will sink in water, while a diet soda can float.

☐ You see the lightning flash before you hear the thunder. This is a result of light moving far more quickly than sound.

☐ Mercury has a unique property to exist as a liquid at room temperature.

☐ Microscopic water creatures generate between 50 and 85 percent of the oxygen on Earth.

☐ Planck time is regarded as the smallest physically meaningful unit of time.

☐ A person could be able to produce enough sound energy to heat one cup of coffee if they were to yell nonstop for eight years, seven months, and six days.

☐ According to Albert Einstein's theory of special relativity, if you are moving faster, you will live longer.

☐ Food tastes can change when traveling via plane because variations in altitude and air pressure can have an impact on our perception of taste and smell.

☐ About two million hydrogen atoms arranged side by side would be required to have a diameter of 0.5 millimeters, or one full stop.

SPORTS & GAME

☐ The sale of frisbees is more than footballs, basketballs, and baseballs, in the USA.

☐ 'USARPS' USA Rock Paper Scissors League is organized every year for the rock-paper-scissors competent.

☐ The four kings in a typical deck of cards have names derived from historical European kings.

☐ Because it seems like the king of hearts is cutting himself in the skull, he is sometimes referred to as the 'suicide king'.

☐ The maximum amount of time ever spent playing a board game is 80 hours.

☐ The total of the numbers on a die's opposing sides is 7.

Baseball

☐ In a major league game, the average lifespan of a baseball is 6 or 7 pitches.

☐ According to the 2023 attendance, around 70 million people attend the baseball Major League every year.

Bowling

☐ Around 3000 BC, there is the oldest evidence of a game resembling bowling from ancient Egypt.

Checkers

☐ The game of checkers started in ancient Egypt, approx 1500 BCE chess was started in India during the Gupta Empire (320–550 CE).

Chess

☐ Both players in chess can play their first four moves in 318,979,564,000 possible ways.

Fidget spinner

☐ By making small movements with your hands and feet called fidgeting, you can burn up to 350 calories a day.

Golf

☐ In golf language, 'Bo Derek' refers to the score of 10 on a single hole. It means completing a hole in 10 strokes.

☐ The US golf ball is slightly different than the UK golf ball. The former has 336 while the latter has 330 dimples on it.

☐ Until the 17th century, wooden balls were used by the kings and royalties to play the earliest golf games.

Jeopardy

☐ In a single Jeopardy game, you can win up to $566,400. However, in a perfectly played final jeopardy round a contestant can win up to $283,200.

Monopoly

☐ Over 480 million people worldwide have been playing the broad game Monopoly for more than 80 years.

☐ Monopoly is so famous in the US that more 'monopoly money' is printed daily than the real US currency.

- [ ] Charles Darrow, in 1933, designed the original Monopoly game board which was circular.

- [ ] American lady Lizzie Magie Philbrick created the most-played board game Monopoly in 1903.

Olympics

- [ ] Canada hosted the Summer Olympics in 1976 and was the only country not to win a gold medal while hosting.

- [ ] An Olympic gold medal is made up of 92.5% silver which is plated with a small amount of gold. It is a rule by the International Olympic Committee.

- [ ] Greece and Australia are the only two countries to participate in the Summer Olympics since the beginning of the modern Olympics in 1896.

- [ ] The Olympic flag represents the colors of every nation's flag as it has red, black, blue, green, and yellow colors on a white background.

Soccer

- [ ] Soccer is regarded as the most popular sport practiced, according to the majority of data.

Swimming

- [ ] Swimming right after having a meal might be uncomfortable but not prohibited.

- [ ] Ahmed Gabr of Egypt broke the record for the deepest free dive into the ocean in 2014 when he dove into the Red Sea to a depth of 702 feet.

- [ ] A courageous and experienced diver reached the lowest point in recorded history, which is roughly 1,090 feet and 4.5 inches (333.33 meters).

Table Tennis

- [ ] Highly skilled table tennis players can hit a ball with their paddle (racket) that may travel at a speed of 160km/hr.

Tennis

- [ ] Before rackets were invented, the original type of tennis was played by striking the ball using bare hands.

Video Game

- [ ] Video games enhance hand-eye coordination, that's why doctors who play video games three hours a week make 37% fewer mistakes in laparoscopic surgery than those who don't play.

- [ ] In a classic arcade Pac-Man game, there are 240 dots that Pac-Man has to eat to finish the level.

- [ ] GTA was originally a car racing game called Race'n'Chase. However, due to a glitch, the police cars started hitting the player's car and this factor became so popular that GTA was born.

- [ ] Minecraft has indeed set an amazing record, making it the best-selling video game ever.

- [ ] With an estimated 3.5 billion supporters worldwide, soccer—also referred to as football in many regions of the world.

- [ ] Every year, more than 200 million ping pong balls are produced at only one factory.

- [ ] Naismith (the inventor) used the only apparatus he had was a peach basket, which is why it's called basketball.

- [ ] The only time golf has ever been played on the moon was when Shepard struck the white golf ball with a homemade club during his lunar mission.

- [ ] In 2010, John Isner and Nicolas Mahut played the longest tennis matches lasted for 11 hours and 5 minutes.

- [ ] At the age of twenty-one years and four months, Mike Tyson accomplished a truly amazing performance in boxing.

- [ ] The National Basketball Association (NBA) record for most points scored in a single game is still held by Wilt Chamberlain's incredible feat.

- [ ] The visual components of games, such as shapes are made with geometry, whereas programming is done with mathematics. Games wouldn't be able to be as graphical and engaging without geometry and mathematics.

- [ ] Every even-numbered year has both the summer and winter Olympics, although not in the same year.

TECHNOLOGY

☐ Floppy disk was used in the past for storing data. Even in today's Microsoft Office programs the 'save' icon is represented by a floppy disk.

☐ There are 4.7 million personal computers in the US that are divided among 89% of the households.

☐ Although the number of landline users is decreasing but still the length of telephone wires across the US is 1,525,000,000 miles.

☐ Deleting SPAM results in productivity loss. Every year $21.6 billion is lost in the USA due to the time spent deleting SPAM.

☐ We can save enough energy by recycling a glass jar to watch TV for 20-30 minutes.

☐ Bhutan has adopted technology very late. It was the only country without telephones in 1980.

☐ The fastest internet speed, as of July 2024, is 402 Tbps. This record is held by Japan's National Institute of Information and Communications Technology.

☐ The startup sound of Windows 95 was composed by Brian Eno, on a Mac.

- [ ] 'Digital Amnesia' or 'Google Effect' is a phenomenon in which people tend to forget the information that can easily be accessed through search engines.

- [ ] By detecting small movements in the cheek muscles of Stephen Hawking, a specialized computer system helped him to communicate one word per minute.

- [ ] The massive search engine was called after the mathematical phrase 'googol', which consists of 1 and 100 zeros.

- [ ] Large units in some nations filter urine and feces from flushed toilet water so that it is safe for human consumption.

- [ ] The approximate cost of a NASA spacesuit is $12,000,000. Out of that amount, 70% is used to make the backpack and control module.

- [ ] In the spam of 63 years, from 1903 to 1966, which is a noteworthy turning point in the history of space travel and aviation.

- [ ] Since the strontium atomic clock measures vibrations using laser beams and quantum gas, it is the most precise timepiece ever created by humans.

- [ ] In 1963, Douglas Engelbart invented the first mouse. This wooden mouse had a button and two wheels to track movement.

- [ ] The Firefox logo represents a red panda rather than a fox. However, the newer version of the logo represents an orange swirl.

- [ ] The most recent data shows that every day almost 3.5 billion Google searches are conducted.

- [ ] Motorola company holds the record of inventing the first ever handheld cellular phone. It was invented in 1973.

- [ ] Nokia started in 1865 as a pulp mill. Later they sold tires, computers, and other electronics and finally became a household name for mobile phones.

TRANSPORTATION

☐ Titanic had two sister ships - RMS Olympic and HMHS Britannic. Olympic served for 24 years, Britannic for a year, and Titanic for just 10 days.

☐ According to the historical records, only 706 people out of 2228 survived when the Titanic sank.

☐ Queen Elizabeth II is a massive ship that moves only a few inches per gallon.

☐ A versatile vehicle used by the army called 'GP' (General Purpose) is most commonly known as Jeep.

☐ In 2001, the number of accidental deaths caused by driving trucks was 799, making it the most dangerous occupation.

☐ The possibility of car theft is probably 1 out of every 230 cars.

☐ Among the Caribbean islands, Cuba is the only one to have a railway system.

- [ ] Mexico City has the world's largest taxi fleet, containing 60,000 taxis.

- [ ] If a fully loaded supertanker is traveling at a normal speed, it will take 20 minutes to stop. However, in emergencies, it can stop in 14 minutes.

- [ ] The modern Boeing 767 is a complex structure made with 3,100,000 individual components.

- [ ] A jumbo jet's tank holds enough fuel that is needed by an average car to drive around the world 4 times.

- [ ] The London Omnibuses are red because the owning company wanted its buses to stand out from the competitors.

- [ ] Around the globe, almost 100 million bicycles are manufactured annually.

- [ ] Cycles have a long history that begin in the early 1800s. Riders had to rely on their balance and leg power to traverse the terrain without the assistance of brakes.

- [ ] The automobile industry is a major global sector that produces more than 150,000 new cars every day.

- [ ] Two jet engines indeed powered the Thrust SSC, the fastest vehicle ever constructed.

- [ ] The Wärtsilä RT-flex96C engine is the largest engine in the world, which is the same as 500 cars driving on the highway simultaneously.

- [ ] There are almost 30,000 parts in a modern car. It's amazing how much of it, about 200-300 components, is devoted to the engine itself.

- [ ] Historical records substantiate the idea that the first electric car was invented in the United States in 1890.

- [ ] Early 19th-century inventors created steam locomotives, which used steam engines to produce power.

- [ ] Motorcycles were referred to as 'Petrol Cycles' before 1894.

- [ ] A longer boat has a higher hull speed because waves travel faster when they are farther apart.

UNEXPLAINED MYSTERIES

☐ A centuries-old book 'Voynich Manuscript' is filled with mysterious illustrations and script. No one could ever de-code the script or understand its meaning.

☐ The exact location of Alexandar the Great's tomb is a mystery. No one knows where it is. However, some people say, it was built in the part of ancient Alexandria which is now partially underwater.

☐ Among the Seven Wonders of the Ancient World, the one that has no archaeological evidence is the Hanging Gardens of Babylon. These gardens were made on terraces with plants hanging from the balconies and walls.

☐ The chances of a baby being born male are slightly higher than a female baby. The expectancy of a baby boy is 51.2%, meaning for every 100 girls 105 boys are born.

☐ Blonde hairs are thinner and finer than dark hair, however, the number of hairs, on the head, increases as the hair color gets lighter.

☐ The Neanderthal had a wider structure than the ancient and modern humans.

- [ ] Studies show that women have a slightly improved sense of hearing than men, especially when it comes to higher frequency sounds.

- [ ] If you are blindfolded, you will walk in a circular pattern rather than straight.

- [ ] Studies show that first-born kids have a better thinking skill and IQ than their siblings.

- [ ] Try to move your foot clockwise and write the number '6' with your hand simultaneously. It's impossible!

- [ ] You yawn for no particular reason. Frequent yawning is an involuntary bodily reflex that you perform without conscious thought.

- [ ] In Australia, the topic of discussion is the feral cats, which have reached sizes similar to those of mountain lions. DNA testing has confirmed that they are feral cats despite their enormous stature.

- [ ] South America's mysterious transparent crystal skulls' origin is unknown, scholars have put up a number of theories as to why they exist.

- [ ] There would have been a great deal of uncertainty and worry in medieval England over the unexplained entrance of two children with green skin and an unidentifiable language.

- [ ] On March 8, 2014, Malaysian Airlines Flight 370 took off from Malaysia. that carried 239 passengers. Despite a thorough search, its location is still unknown.

- [ ] 25 American diplomats working in Cuba reported unexplained health problems. They all blamed a noise they heard. There's still no explanation for the cause.

- [ ] The building of Stonehenge continues to be one of the most mysterious archaeological riddles.

- [ ] The Voynich Manuscript is a mystery handwritten book with over 240 pages of mysterious text that cannot be understood.

- [ ] Children frequently have growing pains. The precise reason behind developing pains is still a mystery.

- [ ] Following an American Civil War combat, a few men saw that their wounds were glowing. Stranger still, the ones that shone appeared to heal faster than the others.

VOCABULARY

☐ 'Durst' was the past tense and past participle of 'Dare' in Old and Middle English, when this irregular verb first appeared.

☐ The definitions of 'Set' in Merriam-Webster's dictionary are over 464, which makes it one of the most flexible and context-dependent words in the English language.

☐ In the English language, 'Almost' is the longest word that has all the letters in alphabetical order.

☐ The longest one-syllable word, in the English language, is, 'Screeched'.

☐ The six-letter word 'rhythm' is the longest in the English language without any vowels.

☐ Hashtag is the most common name for the '#' key. However, its original name is 'Octothorpe'

☐ The Eskimos use more than 15 terms to characterize different types of snow, such as 'apricot snow', 'crisp snow', 'tormenting snow', and 'wind-blown snow'.

☐ To make the shoelace simpler to thread through eyelets, little plastic or metal tips are affixed to the ends of the laces, they are called aglets.

☐ There is a specific name for the dot over the letter 'i', it is called a 'Title'.

☐ A valid phobia known as 'Triskaidekaphobia' refers to an unreasonable fear of the number 13.

☐ Excessive fear of Friday the 13th is a phobia known as 'Paraskevidekatriaphobia'. Depending on the Gregorian calendar, Friday the 13th happens anywhere from 0 to 3 times annually.

☐ The phenomenon where people cannot remember the proper word is called 'Lethologica'.

☐ 'Madam', 'kayak', and 'racecar' are a few examples of words that you can also read backward. Such a word that reads the same both forward and backward is called a palindrome.

☐ Someone who is very interested in the newest rumors, gossip, and news is called a 'Quidnunc' (pronounced kwid-nunk).

☐ 'Month', 'orange', 'silver', and 'purple' are among the unrhymable words, according to English language specialists.

- ☐ You cannot find a word that ends in 'mt', in the English language, except for 'Dreamt'.

- ☐ The term 'Hedonophobia' describes the condition where a person experiences an extreme fear of pleasure.

- ☐ The term 'Canada' originated from an Indian word 'Kanata', meaning 'Village' or 'Settlement'.

- ☐ The only state in the US with a one-syllable name is Maine.

- ☐ There are 10 body parts whose names contain only three letters: jaw, rib, lip, gum, eye, hip, arm, leg, ear, and toe.

- ☐ Some of the words that contain all 5 vowels in order are facetious, abstemious, and arsenious.

- ☐ 'Epizootic' is a term used for 'Epidemic in animal population'.

- ☐ The longest one-word anagram is hydroxydeoxycorticosterones = hydroxydesoxycorticosterone.

- ☐ 'Esposa' is a Spanish word that means 'Wife'. Its plural is 'Esposas', which means 'Wives', however, it has a second meaning too - 'Handcuffs'.

- ☐ There is a no-mobile-phone-phobia called 'Nomophobia'. It is the fear of being away from a mobile phone.

- ☐ In English, the word 'Colgate' means 'Dark gate', while in Spanish, it means 'Go, hang yourself'.

- ☐ The French version of LOL is MDR 'Mort De Rire', which means 'Dying of laughter'.

- ☐ Arithmophobia is a real phobia that affects people who get extremely scared or anxious when they have to deal with numbers or mathematical concepts.

- ☐ A palindrome number is a special kind of numerical sequence in which the sequence reads the same with its digits inverted like 12821.

- ☐ Tonsurephobia, or the unreasonable fear of receiving a haircut, is a legitimate phobia.

- ☐ By definition, a duel is a two-people fight. A truel is a rather rare term that describes a three-person battle.

- ☐ Since the word 'Synonym' specifies a concept of words with identical meanings, it does not itself have a direct synonym.

- [ ] An individual with an illogical fear of eggs is referred to as an oophobic.
- [ ] The initial two letters of the Greek alphabet, alpha, and beta, are the source of the word 'Alphabet'.
- [ ] A person who is knowledgeable in many different fields is known as a polymath.
- [ ] When written vertically, 'NOON' and 'SWIMS' are both palindromes, meaning that they both make sense when turned upside down.
- [ ] There's not a single word that rhymes with 'Orange'.
- [ ] 'Skholē' is a Greek word that means 'Leisure' or 'Free time'. The word 'School' has been derived from this Greek word.
- [ ] A 'Nurdle' is a little bit of toothpaste that gets squeezed onto your toothbrush.
- [ ] An 'Aglet' is a tiny plastic component that is wrapped around the shoelace's end.
- [ ] It is true that one billion years is equal to one 'Giga-year'.
- [ ] Ten years make up a 'Decade'. One 'Century' is 100 years and one 'Millennium' is 1,000 years, and it is used to denote important anniversaries.
- [ ] 'Quindecennial' is a term used for 15th anniversary.
- [ ] The concern that peanut butter will get trapped on the roof of your mouth, causing discomfort and misery, is known as arachibutyrophobia.
- [ ] The plural version is spaghetti, its singular form, spaghetto, is less frequently used in English.
- [ ] Clinophobia is a phobia that affects those who have an excessive fear of falling asleep.
- [ ] The child who looked after the cows was originally called a coward!
- [ ] It's true that the peculiar word for the unreasonable fear of ducks watching you is anataephobia.
- [ ] The letters 'listen' and 'silent' are made from the same letters but their arrangements are different.

WAR & MILITARY

- [ ] During the Battle of Bardia, in 1941, the song 'We are off to see a wizard' acted as a morale booster for the Australian soldiers.

- [ ] The number of people who died in World War II was almost 60 million.

- [ ] Only 23% of Americans between the ages of 17 and 24 years are eligible to serve in the military.

- [ ] To serve in the US military, one must have a High School Diploma. The percentage of high school diploma holders in the US military is 99%, while in the general population, it is only 60%.

- [ ] The Department of Defense is the nation's largest employer with more than 1.3 million people on actively serving, 811,000 National Guard and Reserve members, and 750,000 civilian members.

- [ ] California accommodates the largest veteran population of the USA with 1.7 million prior service members.

- [ ] The number of US presidents who have served in the US military is 31.

- [ ] In 1781, a girl named Deborah Sampson enlisted in the US Army as a man, using the name Robert Shurtleff. However, later her identity was disclosed when she went to a doctor after getting seriously ill.

- [ ] Military families move from one station to another every 2-4 years. This movement is called PCS move - Permanent Change of Station.

- [ ] According to the 2024 report, there are 128 US military bases in almost 55 countries.

- [ ] More than 30 million acres of land, around the globe, is owned by the USA's Department of Defense.

- [ ] North Korea has trained canines as weapons, and the Soviets employed them as suicide bombers during World War II.

- [ ] During WWII, the Germans created 'Goliath tracked mines', which are remote-controlled bombs, and manufactured 7,564 single-use Goliaths.

- [ ] The synthetic fiber Kevlar used in bullet-resistant clothing was created in 1965 by American chemist Stephanie Louise Kwolek.

- [ ] A laser installed on a jet to destroy missiles is known as an airborne laser. The Russians still have two operational laser laboratories, while the United States discontinued its aerial lasers.

- [ ] In 2005, some NASA nerds built a quadrupled military robot called the BigDog. However, the military promptly put the project on hold due to excessive noise from robots.

- [ ] The Japanese dropped hundreds of Fu-Go 'bomb balloons' on the United States during the final nine months of World War II. However, only six Americans died.

- [ ] The Russian and American forces have trained dolphins for a variety of jobs, including bomb detection, because of their high intellect nature.

- [ ] A repeating crossbow known as the Cho-ko-nu was created in China between 475 and 220 BCE, during the Warring States Period. Ten bolts may be fired by it in less than 30 seconds.

- [ ] During the second world war Nazis deliberately killed 6 million European Jews, this event is called Holocaust.

- [ ] Collectively, at every minute, 1 billion tons of water falls on earth when it rains.

- [ ] You are more likely to get stung by a bee on a windy day than on any other day.

- [ ] Fog is nothing but a low cloud. There is actually no difference between fog and cloud besides altitude.

- [ ] Raindrops have different sizes, however, in general, the speed of a falling raindrop varies between 15 and 25 miles per hour.

- [ ] When the dust particles, from the dust storms, get mixed with water droplets in rain clouds, and fall on the Earth, the color of the rain seems to be red.

- [ ] The foggiest place on Earth is the Grand Banks, located off the coast of Newfoundland, Canada.

- [ ] A high ridge on the East Antarctic plateau in Antarctica is said to be the coldest place on Earth. The minimum recorded temperature is -93°C or -135.8°F. in August 2010, a NASA satellite measured that coldest ever temperature.

- [ ] The width of raindrops may vary from 1 – 3mm. With the increasing width the air resistance increases and the shape of the raindrop changes from a sphere to a hamburger bun to a distorted parachute.

- [ ] The windiest US state is South Dakota. Here the winds blow as fast as 21.3 miles per hour.

- [ ] With the average wind speed of 12.9 miles per hour, Delaware becomes the least windy US state.

- [ ] The hurricanes spin anticlockwise in the Northern hemisphere, while in the Southern hemisphere, they spin clockwise.

- [ ] On 10th July 1913, the temperature recorded in Furnace Creek Ranch, California, was 134°F or 56.7°C. In the recorded history, it is the hottest temperature.

- [ ] Sometimes the snowstorms, in Antarctica, are so severe that due to the heavy snowfall and strong winds, you cannot even see your hand. It is called whiteout!

- [ ] 'Black ice' is a layer of transparent ice that forms on roads and pavements. This coating is nearly invisible, slippery, and dangerous.

- [ ] Frogs can sense the changing amount of moisture in the air, and that's why they get noisier just before the rain.

- [ ] According to meteorologists, almost 2000 thunderstorms happen simultaneously around the globe, at any time.

- [ ] The sun needs to be at a 40-degrees angle or less to create a rainbow and this is possible only in the morning or late afternoon.

- [ ] Every second, the light strikes the earth 100 times worldwide, meaning 8.6 million strikes per day!

- [ ] The weight of an average cloud is almost 1.1 million pounds or 500 metric tons.

- [ ] Indeed, hurricanes that originate over the water have a long life—some have been known to last for 10 days or longer.

- Stanley, La Paz, Falkland, and Punta Arenas are the cities with average cold temperatures below 50°F or 10°C. However, there are no records of zero-degree temperatures in these areas, ever.
- The heat from the rays of the sun during the day pushes air upward, creating clouds. Thus, you see more clouds during the day than at night.
- Sandstorm can shallow up a whole city.

- X -

Hello,

Thank you for reading this book. I tried hard to compile 1600+ top-of-the-line facts to satisfy your innate curiosity. If you truly enjoyed this book and found it useful, please take a moment to write a <u>review</u> of it. You can simply scan the following code to leave your review.

Thank you!

Paul Dev

Scan Me

Made in the USA
Las Vegas, NV
07 December 2024

13559560R00077

Thank you

for choosing our Vision Board Clip Art Book

As a special GIFT
I am offering you a complimentary guide to download.

This guide is designed to help you confidently create your vision board, set SMART goals, and embrace unlimited possibilities for your dreams.

Open the camera on your phone
(as if you're going to take a photo)
Hold the phone on the QR CODE below then
a link will appear on your screen
Tap on the link to get your FREE GUIDE

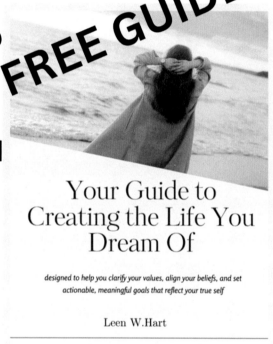

FREE GUIDE

Your Guide to Creating the Life You Dream Of

designed to help you clarify your values, align your beliefs, and set actionable, meaningful goals that reflect your true self

Leen W.Hart

Much Love
Leen

Made in the USA
Las Vegas, NV
02 January 2025

15758269R00031